PLE
REMEMBER ME
AS I WAS

A Memoir
of Living with
PCA Alzheimer's

Valerie Blumenthal

PLEASE REMEMBER ME AS I WAS

I was told by my doctor that I was suffering
from stress; but I knew otherwise.

This is my story of what it feels like to have a rare
form of Alzheimer's. In order to recount it I have
used voice recognition software.

As, little by little I am deprived of my faculties,
I am rendered completely illiterate.
It is a cruel trick to play on a novelist.

I hope that this book will resonate
with all who might read it.

Reviews of Valerie Blumenthal's previous books.

*"Valerie Blumenthal writes beautifully about the
mother/daughter relationship, hidden secrets and
Alzheimer's in her latest novel set in Italy."*
Tina Betts, literary agent on **The Lupo Stick**

*"Valerie Blumenthal explores her protagonist's
dilemma with sympathy and tact, producing a very
readable novel which makes some thoughtful
points about the nature of maternal love."*
The Times on **Saturday's Child**

*"Wise novel ... Shrewdly observed
and lit by comic compassion."*
She Magazine on **Kempton's Journey**

Also by Valerie Blumenthal

To Anna - About Whom Nothing Is Known

The Colour of Her Days

Homage to Sarah

Knowing Me

Kempton's Journey

Chasing Eagles

Saturday's Child

Moth in Amber (Published in Holland)

The Lupo Stick

*This book is dedicated to my beloved
husband, Christopher Yeates.*

*I could not have written
this book without you.*

*With thanks and much love,
also to my darling daughter Ingrid
and my brother Adrian Blumenthal.*

ABOUT THE AUTHOR

Valerie Blumenthal is the author of nine critically acclaimed novels, several of which have been widely translated. Her novel *Saturday's Child* sold in the region of a million copies worldwide. She has written features for the *Times, Telegraph, Mail on Sunday* and the *Oxford Times,* published several short stories and for four years taught creative writing in a high security men's prison.

Valerie was a third of the way through writing *The Lupo Stick,* when she was diagnosed with PCA (Posterior Cortical Atrophy), a rare form of Alzheimer's, which strikes at a younger age. Writing *The Lupo Stick* had been a labour of love, but also one that had been fraught with frustration, as her condition altered over the six years it took to write.

Valerie's situation now is such that she needs help with the simplest, everyday things, however, she retains her sense of humour and positive outlook.

PLEASE REMEMBER ME AS I WAS

Author: Valerie Blumenthal
Front Cover Illustration: Valerie Blumenthal
Publisher: Paula Keogh

Published by Ellis Editions, London

Ellis Editions

www.ellisbooks.co.uk
hello@ellisbooks.co.uk

ISBN 978-1-9196114-3-3
eISBN 978-1-9196114-4-0

ACKNOWLEDGEMENTS

I would also like to dedicate this collection of my memoirs and memories to Alzheimer's Research UK, a charity very close to my heart. Alzheimer's Research UK is the UK's leading dementia research charity dedicated to causes, diagnosis, prevention, treatment and cure. They are providing hope to people like me, loved ones and families and I will continue to support their brilliant work.

www.alzheimersresearchuk.org

CONTENTS

PLEASE
REMEMBER ME
AS I WAS

A Memoir
of Living with
PCA Alzheimer's

Valerie Blumenthal

ONE – A DREAM

"No! No!"

I wake from my nightmare, writhing in distress. My entire body is heaving from my grief. I can barely breathe. Tears drench my pillow. "What's wrong, what's wrong darling?"

My sleep befuddled husband is instantly awake, his arms are around me now, and I sob into them, clutching him, as he attempts to console me.

"I dreamt you no longer loved me."
I manage to gasp, like a pitiful child.

He smiles gently then, stroking my face.
"But it was just a dream", he tries to sooth me.

"And I will always love you," he insists.

But the cold stare of my dream lingers, piercing through me, and I shake my head in knowing sorrow.

"But, as I get worse and worse, and I am no longer me, you will come to resent me," I tell him.

He clenches his jaw, in denial. "You will feel guilty. You won't be able to help it, and you could not be blamed for that." I tell him.

"His eyes are moist with unshed tears.
"You will always be you," he says in a choked voice.

And he grips my hand. "We will face this together.
I love you, now, go to sleep."

Oh, if only; if only.

I listen to his breathing as it changes and he exhales
in little squeaks. The darkness embraces me;
images swim before my eyes.

*The tiny figure of a child flitting by. Twinkling feet,
striped puffed sleeves and ankle socks. Through the
lens of my vision, and the pale pencil line of my past,
she dances by me. Linked by long-gone, tender hands
through the heath's tall, bleached grass, she skips, she
smiles without recognition, then fades through the
slits of my hankering eyes.*

Other images: the little girl has become an adult;
she is galloping on her horse, and the wind is in
her long hair. She is bare headed, and wears no hard-hat;
she is laughing with the joy of her freedom.

The images waver and fade. I succumb to my tiredness,
and snuggle into Chris's warmth. He murmurs something
I cannot decipher the jumbled words and I wrap my cold
toes around his feet.

It is impossible for me to say when the brain gremlins
first made themselves apparent. Little by little they have
invaded my life, snipping away gleefully, in a pitiless game
of subtraction. They have a warped sense of humour.

There was a time when my brain and I were on good terms; after all, we had known each other from birth. We were cosy bedfellows, privy to each other's thoughts and secrets. My brain is me, and I am my brain; but we have been wrenched apart, confounded, left flailing and bewildered.

PCA or Posterior Cortical Atrophy, to use its full name, is a form of Alzheimer's, where the back part of the brain is withered. It is this 'zone' which is responsible for vision, motor skills and sequential awareness. It is considered to be rare, though I have my doubts. I believe it is misdiagnosed or undiagnosed; not surprising, considering the weird raft of apparently disparate symptoms. Trust me to have some rare disease that no one has heard of - but then, I was always perverse.

Living with PCA is akin to living with a poltergeist: you go to look for something, only to find it in a completely different place from where you believed you had put it. If I had to describe what it is like to have PCA, I think I would have to liken it to suffering from very severe dyslexia, coupled with dyspraxia, dyscalculia, and spatial awareness. Worst of all is the fact that PCA causes you to become completely illiterate. I am a published novelist; writing has been my life, and my livelihood, for many years; PCA has put an end to this. It is surely a cruel trick to play on a writer. The brain gremlins have excelled themselves; I can imagine them laughing around a table, and toasting their success. With the passage of time the symptoms of PCA become ever more extreme and daily life, ever more of a challenge; the simplest of tasks are out to thwart me and defy me. Going to the shops, making phone calls, putting a plug in, wrapping a present, laying the table, handling small change. All these become absurdly complicated. You go to sit where there is no seat and end up on a strangers lap; you go to the post office, where a snaking queue is causing tempers to fray, and you make a beeline for the front - prompting mass fury. You go into your neighbours' garden, become disorientated, and cannot find your way out; it is as if you have been spun round and round. PCA creeps up on you with the stealth of a thief. Generally it kidnaps you in your fifties or sixties, when you should still feel at your peak. Now the brain gremlins and I are at war. PCA quashes the free spirit in you. As the disease progresses, so, increasingly, it chips away at your confidence, and deprives you of your of independence. The second you step out through the front door, particularly when going somewhere unfamiliar, you feel vulnerable, exposed, and the tension rises in you.

Relinquishing your independence is a hard thing to do, for a once-upon-a-time Free Spirit. Inside you sometimes want to yell out that you were too young for this. But finally I have capitulated to the comforting reassurance of my husband's arm, and allow him to shepherd me, across the road, and to navigate the pavement's hazardous straits.

As you would expect with Alzheimer's, there are good days, and not such good days. On a good day I feel energised, as though I would be capable of tackling almost anything. I can converse quite normally, and if you were meeting me for the first time you would be unlikely to realise anything was wrong. Of course, this can be deceptive; without warning, the words might slide away from me, and I am left floundering in embarrassment.

PCA is a weird disease, to say the least. You see - yet you don't see. It is as though your perceived vision is lagging behind the actuality. Without your being aware, your eyes are ambulant, continually moving, and you have to adjust your vision accordingly. Judging distance is impossible, you focus on an object, but a second later you are unable to locate it; when finally you do locate it again you see it perfectly; but only for an instant. And then this image, too, disappears. I wish I could explain this more succinctly, but PCA is so contradictory, and I am unable to do so.

TWO – MY MOTHER

The year was 2012. My eighty-nine year old mother
was terminally ill with Parkinson's and dementia.

It is a mild, spring day, and my mother and I are
circling round the garden at a snail's pace.
She leans heavily on a walking frame, gripping it
so tightly from the effort that the veins of her fingers
protrude like claws. She had such beautiful hands once;
long, elegant fingers without a blemish.

As we walk I point out various things which might be
of interest to her: the red kite in the distance; buds that
had burst into flower overnight; the clacking sound of
a disturbed pheasant. She disregards my efforts.

"I want to go home now," she tells me.
"It's a very long way home." I do not contradict her.
Slowly, painfully, we re-trace our steps.

Back indoors I settle her in her usual chair, and she slumps
into it, as though she has just completed a marathon.
Absently, I glance at the large clock on the kitchen wall;
I had bought it for her a few months previously, to enable
her to read it more easily; now, however, I found that I was
unable to decipher any of the digits. Only by squinting
was I finally able to tell the time. It remains etched in my
memory: 12:10. Had that been the beginning?

Disconcerted I made tea for us both, and switched on the
television for my mother. She was staring at me in a strange
manner, as though she were troubled by something.

Ignoring the television, she continued to gaze at me, frowning in that same, assessing manner. Then, in a lucid, gentle, tone, she said, "Darling, I do hope you're not getting the same illness that I've got".

I was stunned. What had prompted this remark? Had I said or done anything stupid, without my realising it? She and I had always been exceptionally close; had she sensed something in my demeanour? Had the remark been prescient in some way. I shall never know.

There is so much I remember about my mother: her beauty, of course; her kindness; her humour; her wisdom; her pride in me when I became a published novelist; and - much more recently - her stoic bravery when my father, the only man she had ever loved, died. He had been a brilliant, charismatic man, of great intellect and humour. I commented to her one day that she had not cried.

"I can't cry. I have never been able to cry." She tried to explain. "I was brought up to have a stiff upper lip, and not to talk about my feelings. It was a different era then."

We played dominoes together, and snakes and ladders. I bought her a writing pad, so she could write about her feelings; but it remained untouched. I watched her condition deteriorate. One day I broached the subject of death: did she believe in anything? Was she afraid at all, I had asked her?

"Oh no darling," she replied, with conviction, "I shall see your daddy again and everyone I love."

It gives me such comfort to know that she had not been afraid.

It has only just struck me that I have a kind of affinity with my mother: we have both experienced dementia, and I recognise myself in her. If anything, I feel even closer than I did when she was alive. I understand her. I know what she went through. I hope I can be as stoic as she was.

In the earlier stages of her illness, I used to see her at least four times a week and I would phone her twice a day. On the other days, I had organised for a carer to come. I recall an amusing incident: I had phoned in the morning, to speak to her; the carer had passed the telephone to my mother, then left us to it. "I can't talk now," came my mother's surprisingly youthful voice, sounding agitated. "I'm very busy."

"Oh", I said, trying to sound nonchalant.
"I'm sorry to disturb you; what are you doing"

"I'm selling the house," my mother said. At this point she was in her usual chair, and was watching television. I thought quickly: "I mustn't disturb you then." I paused, "Are you by any chance watching one of those interesting property programs," I asked. "Yes darling," she affirmed, "it's really interesting, I must go." And she hung up.

A day after this little incident, my mother requested that I read to her. The book that she asked for was one of my own, and had been her favourite. I made her comfortable, and started to read. I stopped, almost immediately. The words were dancing before my eyes, like witches. I knew the beginning by heart, and began again. I made another attempt; but the same thing happened. I could not read a word. What was happening to me? I could not read my own novel, which had once meant so much to me.

Meanwhile, my mother had fallen asleep anyway.

GHOSTS

In this soulless place of lost dreams
and fragmented memories,
These are the ghosts of my future,
from which there is no escape.
With gentle cruelty the past nudges me.
Your turn soon, it whispers.
Trembling fingers, like broken wings,
stretching out for help:
What's wrong dear? What do you want?
The ghost does not reply. It wants too much.
Most of all it yearns for youth.
And in this sterile place of lost dreams and blank faces,
the television plays on and on and on without remorse.
But from a far corner of the room comes a faintest of stirs;
I notice, then, the tiny, wizened, figure; a smile flickers on
the edge of her lips, like a tiny beacon.
For a moment it seems as though
she is embraced by a halo of light
Is she remembering the many times she lay in a damp,
coital pleasure, and she would turn to him beside her,
with illuminated eyes?
Then the light dims,
and the ghost of my future tip toes away.

THREE – A WALK

It is early autumn, and you can smell the change of the season in the crisp air, there is a unique, sweet scent, of grass and soil, coupled with burnt wood from a recent bonfire. As I walk with my dog, the last of summer's sun is so bright that I have to shield my eyes with my hand. It is a golden landscape.

We walk towards the nearby nature reserve; the tall trees cast shadows and reflections beneath my feet, and I tread carefully to avoid tripping. I know every inch of this terrain and am unconcerned; in addition, I always have my phone with me. My dog, a Lassie collie, is not on a lead, and stops every few seconds to sniff at various smells, or to greet one of his friends - before bounding back to me. Today, however, after we have walked a couple of miles, I look round for Elgar, but he is nowhere to be seen. I call, and call him without success. My heart is racing. Frantically, I continue to call. I don't know how long he has been gone - it feels like hours, but in all probability it was no more than five or ten minutes, when suddenly he appears, panting, and wagging his tail. My hand is shaking to such an extent, that I can barely fasten his lead. We resume our walk then turn off the footpath, and head for the brook. After a while it occurs to me that the brook is nowhere in sight; we have been walking for ages, and the path has narrowed. I pass the odd person - a runner, a cyclist, a woman with a baby in a pram - but nobody do I recognise. The sun is ever brighter, and I wish I had worn sunglasses. I realise I am lost. Dismayed, I gaze around me. The many twists and turns, coupled with the blinding light, further confuses me. I feel as though I have been spun round.

I try to think logically. Surely I cannot be far from somewhere familiar I tell myself. And turn back and we walk in the opposite direction. Now, the landscape changes as fields of stubble stretch before me. I feel as though I am marooned, caught up in a surreal nightmare. Then I hear voices and half a dozen cyclists appear. I flag them down, waving my white stick, and they put on their brakes, with a great deal of squeaking. I explain my predicament, making light of the situation, whilst within me I feel embarrassed, foolish. The men are so kind and think they must use sensed my distress despite my attempts at humour. Two of them had GPS Apps on their phones, and I gave them my postcode. They argue between themselves, laughing and joking; "you should have asked your Lassie dog to find your way home, "one of them says. After several minutes of further discussion, they manage to put me straight, and slowly cycle alongside me - oh joy - I recognise where I am.

I thank them profusely; I try to sound dignified and intelligent, I explain about the dog going missing.
I explain that I have been ill, but I cannot bring myself to admit that I have Alzheimer's. Why cannot I tell the truth? Where is the shame in having Alzheimer's?

When finally I am home and my concerned husband has ceased to chastise me, and has made me a cup of tea, I cry. And now, several hours later, I recall how my dog had attempted to go in a different direction, from that which I had taken. I remember his expression; he had seemed bewildered, reluctant to continue walking.

Clearly my Lassie dog had realized we were going the wrong way. If something like this were to happen again I would put my faith Elgar.

A JOTTING

This morning, I am disturbed from my writing, by an extraordinary cacophony of sound. I ran to the window. Directly outside a skein of Canada Geese was flying over the house. There must have been more than a dozen of them, 20 or 30, honking noisily, their wings outstretched as they flew south, seeking gentler climes. Amongst them were a few stragglers; I dare say that the geese would have been exhausted by their thousand mile journey. They come to the same spot every year: the farm a mile or so from where I now stand. As they land and settle, they disperse.

I feel so privileged to have witnessed this sight. I can only marvel at this incredible feat of endurance, in order to escape the freezing Arctic.

FOUR – MEMORIES

I am at the stage now where I am continually besieged by
memories. They do not leave me alone: there is no pattern
to them; no sequence; no rhyme nor reason.

If I close my eyes, I can see anyone; be anyone;
conjure up whomever I wish.

And all at once I am taken back to childhood. My older
brother, Adrian, and his best friend Anthony were bored
one day, and they decided that, for want of anything
better to do, they would trawl the through the telephone
directory, in search of strange surnames. To their delight,
they happened across the name Smelly. They let out
screeches of laughter. There were eleven people with
that name; and, barely able to control their mirth,
the boys rang each one in turn.

"Are you smelly", they demanded to each baffled person,
"then have a bath", they shrieked, before slamming down
the hand set.

My brother would have been about fourteen at the time;
I was five years younger; but I recall that day so clearly,
and I am laughing at the memory as I dictate this.

I can remember the faces of friends and family; countries
I have visited; and the beautiful dogs I have owned.
How can I ever be bored, with such a cornucopia of choice,
from which to pluck?

I was fiercely independent, and loved to explore new places. I would ride my Anglo Arab horse bareback; my then, German Shepherd, would follow alongside us. That is who I was; but that was then. I long for the *"then"*.

I loved that horse. I was the only person who could ride him because he was so naughty; but he and I had an incredible rapport, and even though he was highly strung, I could always control him. We had each other for twenty three years; he died in his field at the age of nearly thirty. I had dreamt about his death the previous night and it was exactly as my dream had been. He was buried in a friend's beautiful orchard.

FIVE – STRANGE HAPPENINGS

But now I think I should go back in time a little and explain how I discovered that I had Posterior Cortical Atrophy.

I am a mother, a grandmother, and a wife.
Ours is a close-knit family, and I have been blessed in many ways. Over the years, I suppose you could say I have had my share of health issues; I have overcome breast cancer, and hip operations. These apart, I would consider myself as being fit, and, dare I say it, youthful.

I was finally diagnosed with Posterior Cortical Atrophy nearly five years ago, in reality I am certain that I had had PCA for several years before. All the signs had been there, but, of course, I would not have recognised their significance then.

I had always liked driving, and my old MGB and I had enjoyed many adventures together over the years. With the rear seat folded down, my German Shepherd had the seat all to himself, and would sit upright, King of the Road. We explored remote parts of Britain, and becoming lost would make it all the more fun. If it was raining, I would don a man's hat, as the roof leaked.

I had my beautiful car for about four years; but a car's purpose is to go from A to B; mine went from A. It was one of those cars you would see stationary, lonely, at the side of the road, the hazard lights blinking to alert people that it had broken down. I used to dread traffic jams, and I would watch the needle creeping towards the red, as I revved the engine frantically, without success.

With heavy heart I replaced it with something mundane and reliable, which went from A as well as B. And for several years I drove my ordinary, unexciting, car without mishap. But then, I became aware something strange was happening, and I could no longer disregard this: every time that I stepped into the car I would tense up, but I could not comprehend why. I realised that I was finding it difficult to concentrate. I was mystified; I'd always been such a confident driver. Now, however, road signs leapt out at me confusingly, and I would find myself swerving to avoid oncoming traffic. I was unable to work out how to position the car in relation to the road, and equally, I was becoming increasingly anxious.

I took out the radio and CD player so as not to be distracted. I went for an eye test; but it revealed nothing unexpected. I told myself that this had to be psychological, and that, really I had to pull myself together and stop being so silly.

Over a period of two years, I got through about half a dozen wing mirrors, due to clipping oncoming cars. There would be an almighty bang, followed by furious hooting, as yet another wing mirror flew off.

"It wasn't my fault." I would sheepishly tell the mechanic, as he fitted yet another wing mirror.

"Yeah yeah," he responded knowingly - we had known each other for several years. "Don't be sarcastic to the hand that feeds you," I quipped.

My dread of driving worsened. I used to teach creative writing in a men's prison, and I imagined myself being incarcerated like one of them. I could picture myself in the dock, being sentenced for dangerous driving.

After any journey I took, I would arrive at my destination trembling and perspiring, and it would take me some time for my equilibrium to be restored. Even the dog did not like my driving; he had to be bribed with treats before he would finally clamber, reluctantly, into my car. When it came to parking, I would drive round and round in search of a space big enough for a stretch limo. And then there was the day, when I found the perfect spot, with plenty of clearance.

"Great," I thought, with relief, and I started to accelerate into the space, before anyone else could. I stopped abruptly, just in time. The empty space had not been empty after all; it was already occupied by a low sports car. My skewed vision had failed to register its presence. I remember feeling sick with shock, and I could barely breathe.

Our narrow driveway had become a patchwork of zigzags and criss-crossings, as a result of my efforts to reverse. My long suffering husband suggested I take a refresher course for driving, in order to restore my confidence. I was not keen: I knew that this would result in having to take another driving test, and of course, I would have failed. Instead, I took myself off to the doctors.

"I think I might have something like my mother has, I told my very nice GP. And as I spoke, I recalled my mother's

27

words – I hope you're not getting what I have, darling – she had said, regarding me with that fixed stare.

My doctor raised a sceptical eyebrow.

"What makes you think that," he asked.

"Little things," I replied, "just little things. It's hard to describe," I told him.

"Try," he encouraged me.

I explained to him about my driving, and about my strange experience when I couldn't read to my mother. I pre-empted what I knew would have been his next question: "And yes," I said, "I had an eye test only recently, and it was fine. And there are other things," I continued, "I went to pay the carer on behalf of my mother the other day, and I couldn't do it. I couldn't fill out a cheque. I couldn't work out the order of things." And I cringed, anew thinking about it.

My GP considered me for a minute or so. "I don't believe you have dementia," he said. "You are too young, and too lucid. In my opinion, you are suffering from stress."

"I was born stressed," I joked.

He did not smile. "You've had a lot on your plate, lately," he continued, "what with your cancer, and your ill mother."

"But this is different. It feels different from anything," I insisted. His eyes were sympathetic.

"I would recommend you take a course of anti-depressants," he said. He was about to prescribe them but I declined them.

I returned home, despondent. I continued to drive.

A year had passed. My mother had died and I was finding my new novel, *The Lupo Stick*, increasingly difficult to write. I kept losing my way round the keyboard, and when I did locate the letters they would leap about. Progress was agonisingly slow. On a good day I might manage to write one hundred and fifty words. Frequently, I would be in tears of frustration, and many were the times that I almost gave up in despair.

One extraordinary coincidence which I have, so far, omitted to mention is that I had conceived the idea of *The Lupo Stick* long before I was diagnosed. In my novel the main character has Alzheimer's.

I was completely baffled by what was happening to me. Nothing seemed to make sense, and it was a lonely time. My very understanding husband could not comprehend why I was unable to see objects that were in front of my nose.

Here, is how a typical conversation between us might go: "Have you seen my mug," I might ask.

"It's there, in front of you," he'd reply, frowning.

"Where?" I would say, casting about the room.

"Why can't you see it; it's there in front of you."

And finally I would see it; it was so obvious, why, indeed could I not see it?

... And I used to be a whiz at backgammon. I would always beat my husband, which, must have been very galling for him. But he started to win, three times in succession, and then again.

"I'm starting to get the hang of this," he said, gloating. And then he accused me of cheating, because I had jumped two places over his men.

I realised then, that I couldn't read the dice.

We stopped playing backgammon.

SIX – CHOIR

I have always loved music. I trained as a classical singer,
and played the piano. I particularly like to play Chopin.
One evening, after a boozy girls get together, I suggested
that I start a women's choir. Nothing heavy, I quickly
reassured them, when there were several groans. It would
be a social gathering too, and people could bring wine
if they wished. My little choir grew. I would pluck people
from everywhere. When I met anyone on a dog walk,
I would accost them and ask if they would be interested
in joining my choir. There and then, in the street, I would
get them to sing three or four notes, to make sure they
had a reasonable voice. Everyone loved the choir;
crammed, as we all were, in my living room.
My then German Shepherd, aptly named Mozart,
would lie amongst us, taking up further space.

There would be much hilarity and shrieking, and a few
protestations when they argued that I was being too
ambitious. The songs were a mixture of folk, classical,
and popular, and these were usually in three or four parts,
which I arranged myself. We used to go into old people's
homes to sing, and the residents would join in;
it was heart-warming and, at times moving.

We had five rewarding years, but the brain gremlins
had their own plans. Let's prevent her from being able
to read music, they shrilled, squealing with excitement at
the prospect. And that was the end of my lovely little choir.

We had all become close during the interim years, and
the disbanding of the choir was a sad time. For me it also

served to emphasise the mysterious changes in myself. I seemed to spend my life bluffing, in order to cover up the gaffes that I repeatedly made; the obvious, and easiest, was to pretend I needed new reading glasses, but after a while that began to wear thin. Meanwhile driving was becoming ever more of a nightmare for me and my capabilities were fast diminishing.

Once again I paid a visit to the doctor. And once again, he told me I was suffering from stress.

WRAPPED VIEWS

*Drinking weak coffee
To the mewing of the peewits
Circling over the torpid lake
In disappointment.
How I hate the small wrapped butters,
Sugar cubes and flocked wallpaper,
Discreet whispering
And cheerless sautéed potatoes
Of British hotels,
With their views of smug golf courses,
Usurpers of fields of fritillary;
And the barn has become a clubhouse
And the owl has fled.*

SEVEN – STEPS

Steps came next. Oh God, steps. Wiggly steps, uneven steps, tall steps, short steps, wide steps, narrow steps; all existed for the sole purpose of tripping me up. I had developed a phobia of them, and they took on the proportions of Everest. Going up stairs or steps was not a problem for me - I was like a mountain goat, but going down was another matter. As for escalators - horrible things, I confronted them with dread in my heart. At that time I was going to London frequently in order to visit my daughter; this necessitated taking the underground. I remember, only too well, waiting for the hoards of commuters to rush past me without thought. Eventually, summoning up courage, I would totter onto the escalator. Sometimes the heel of my shoe would become trapped between the treads; panicked, I would wrench it free.

I recall an incident: it was Chris's birthday, and I had treated him to a slap up meal at a posh restaurant. Everything was perfect: the gourmet food, the beautiful Manor House itself, with its antique furnishings and paintings, and after, the meal itself, the delicious *petits fours*.

I went then, to pay the bill. I ascended the plush red staircase without a thought; however, I turned and was confronted with the problem of my descent. There were just four wide steps for me to negotiate but there was no rail for me to grab. Gingerly, with a fixed smile, I commenced my passage… In front of all the other diners, I tripped, and landed on my backside. All I could do, under the circumstances, was to pick myself up, and

33

make an appropriate joke about having had one to many. But within me, I did not feel like laughing; I felt humiliated and just wanted to run from the building, and to cry.

EIGHT – DOGS

The benefits of pets, in particular dogs, have been well documented and proven. And in my experience humans and dogs have always had a symbiotic relationship, and truly, dogs do seem to have the ability to read their owners' mind. In the case of Alzheimer's, it is quite extraordinary to see a patient's face light up at the sight of a dog being brought into a room. I have seen this transformation several times, including with my own mother. For the moment my cognitive function remains largely unimpaired; but, as the years pass, this will inevitably change, and I know that I will always need – not just want, but need – a dog by my side.

Over the years, I have owned six dogs: four German Shepherds, one Irish Wolfhound, and, currently, a Rough Coat Collie. They have all been special in their individual ways; all have had names of composers. My most recent German Shepherd was Mozart, whom I briefly mentioned earlier. He and I had been a team; it was as if he could read my mind. As soon as Chris vacated the bed in the morning, Mozart would spring on, in Chris's place and would snuggle up to me. He would wriggle as close as possible: "wormy to mummy," I would say, and he understood what that meant. As the years passed, and he became less athletic, his beautiful eyes shone with a cataract gaze. I would hug him to me; he smelt of biscuits and soil. Sometimes I can still conjure up that scent of his. I can recall autumnal days and wet, muddy walks; we would return home, filthy and wet. Mozart's paws resembled bars of chocolate. He knew the score, and lay in wait, as I unravelled the hose, which was jagged with bite marks from his teeth. His amber eyes took on that wild look that he reserved specifically for the hose. He would leap and dance about, and we would go round and round in a tangle of hosepipe. I would end up as drenched as him. When I turned off the hose, he was instantly calm and he would proffer each paw in turn, to be dried.

I still miss him, even after one and a half years.

German Shepherds are a unique breed; combined intelligence and loyalty, coupled with their lupine beauty, and sense of fun, makes them irresistible to own. However, it has to be said that they are not easy dogs; they require constant stimulation, and in this respect they are almost akin to children; they crave love and attention, and their dominant nature requires firm handling from puppyhood. They are constantly alert, and at the ready. Also, one must take into consideration their very large size.

After much soul searching I was forced to admit to myself that, due to my Alzheimer's, any subsequent dog I may have in the future, would need to be both calm and biddable.

Enter Elgar.

Rough Coat Collies are a sweet-natured and gentle breed. Now that he is fully matured, he is about the size of a large Labrador, and stunning to look at; because he is so fiery everyone who passes comments, and goes to him, particularly children. I like to think that Mozart would have approved, and I imagine them playing together. Meanwhile, Elgar is already developing his own personality: he has learnt to tilt his head to one side in recognition of a familiar word; he loves being groomed, and emits little grunting sounds of pleasure whilst I brush him. One of his strangest habits is to click his teeth together when he is excited, and he sounds like a rapacious alligator; apparently this is a typical trait of the breed.

One of his most eccentric traits is his fear of shiny floor surfaces. He used to run up and down the stairs, and loved coming into our bedroom, where he would sleep. Then, almost overnight he developed a seemingly irrational fear of slippery floors. This is inconvenient, to put it mildly.

A while ago, we needed to go to the bank. Mozart had always come with us, in the past, and the staff had made a great fuss of him; I thought it would be a good idea to introduce Elgar to them. Elgar, Chris, and myself walked up the road, and turned into the bank. We walked through the automatic doors, across the carpeted interior; Elgar's tale was wagging. All was well to begin with but then he spotted the six foot high advertising placard obstructing his path, and stopped dead in his tracks. To go any further he would be obliged to go across the shiny wood flooring. He backed away as though he were in mortal danger, trying to retreat, making for the door; however, the door was closed. I could see the panic in his eyes. We tried cajoling him but he flatly refused to budge. The bank manager, a dog lover, came over to us to investigate the problem, I explained our predicament. The manager seemed remarkably unsurprised, as though this sort of thing were a regular occurrence in. He was a tall man, and laughing, he said, "no problem". He lifted the unwieldy placard to one side, as though it weighed nothing. Now that he was no longer obstructed, Elgar was able to walk across the carpet as if nothing had occurred. His reward was a dog treat. Finally, we were then able to deal with the business in hand.

And now, listening to what I have just dictated, I am struck, suddenly, by the similarities between Elgar's apparently irrational phobia shiny surfaces, and my own, equally irrational phobia of steps. Oh my poor boy.
I know how you feel.

A TRIBUTE TO MY DOG, MOZART

He is old now, my beautiful dog
His eyes gleam with a cataract gaze;
A translucent mirror, into the depth of his soul.
In human years he has overtaken me,
But he makes no concession to age.
I wish I could share his nonchalance,
His casual disregard, for pitiless time;
A kind of immortality.
And meanwhile, as I muse, he sleeps by my feet,
Curled in a lupine heap,
And now, replete from his walk,
His pricked ears twitch as he squeaks in his sleep.
His dreams are beyond my reach.
My somnambulant guardian;
My beautiful dog.

NINE – BREAKTHROUGH

Yet another year had passed. Somehow, I was still managing to bumble along, holding up impatient customers in the supermarket; dithering when it came to paying, yet I could do nothing about it, and I felt mortified. I felt insecure in every sense of the word, and I was weary from putting on a brave face; weary from all that this entailed. Writing my novel had ceased to give me any pleasure, as I stumbled about on my laptop.

I recall driving back from the train station in full light, when dusk was just replacing daylight; I was driving at about 20 miles an hour, and everyone was hooting at me, or yelling obscenities through open windows. There was a loud jolt as the car's wheel hit the curb. Heart racing, I put the hazard lights on, and continued my perilous journey, at a snail's pace. When I finally arrived home, I burst into tears.

That same evening, by sheer chance, Chris and I were watching television, when an old documentary about Terry Pratchett came on. We watched with growing disbelief, and turned to each other. I could barely contain my excitement.

"Are you thinking the same as I am?" I asked.

I felt vindicated. There was no doubt in my mind: I had the same form of Alzheimer's that had afflicted Terry Pratchett. No longer would I be fobbed off with the usual diagnosis of stress. But, first things first. I booked an appointment with the ophthalmologist; the earliest availability was in a fortnight, and I waited impatiently. When the time itself arrived, I could hardly contain my anxiety.

The ophthalmologist's was running late, which only served to make me more nervous. Then finally I was called in into the waiting room after the usual, obligatory, pleasantries, I came straight to the point. "I don't think there is anything wrong with my eyes," I explained, "It is as though the messages aren't getting through to my brain; but I need to eliminate the possibility of macular degeneration."

He gave me an extensive examination; I could hardly read any of the letters on the wall in front of me and when it came to the "white dot" test, I failed it dismally. He sat back in his swivel chair, and assessed me for a moment or two.

Then he gave a little nod. "Well I can't find anything significantly wrong with your eyes," he told me. "You should be seeing a lot better than you are. I think you are right, and that this is, indeed, something brain related. I shall write to your GP accordingly."

Another trip to the doctor.

This time he greeted me with a weary curtness, as though I was wasting his time. I heard myself stammering in my effort to explain why I had needed to consult an ophthalmologist.

"I'm certain that I have what Terry Pratchett has," I said. "There was this documentary, and honestly, it could have been me."

The Doctor's features softened. "Look, you know what
I think," he said. 'But if it puts your mind at rest,
then I will refer you to a neurologist."

"It will get me off your back at least," I joked.

"You said it, not me," he said, deadpan.

He asked if I had a preference, regarding the specialist;
I suddenly remembered then, and felt a jolt of pain in
my stomach: "I should like to use the same one as my
late mother's," I told him. I could feel tears welling
up as I spoke.

Upon seeing my mother's neurologist again, I was taken
right back. I had come to know him well over the years:
there were the same pictures of his family on the walls;
the same photograph of a barn owl in flight; the same
messy pile of books in the corner of the room.

For a few minutes we talked about my mother.

"She was always so gracious," the neurologist said.

"Yes, she was," I agreed.

"But now, it's over to you," he continued.
"Tell me what's been going on with you?"

I poured out everything, as succinctly as I could,
while he made notes, nodding from time to time
in a thoughtful way.

41

"Aha, aha he would say." He asked me several basic questions then; and I realised he was testing me. I felt self-conscious, and a little foolish.

"Maybe my GP is right. Maybe it's just stress after all," I ventured.

He shook his head emphatically. "No, I think you're right, and I would like to refer you to a clinical psychologist that I know, to see what he makes of it. In all probability, you will need to have a brain scan."

My pulse was racing; at last I was being taken seriously. I could cope with anything, apart from uncertainty.

The clinical psychologist was a tall, taciturn, man with a serious demeanour; and I could not begin to guess what is thoughts were. Despite this, there was something reassuring about his demeanour. I felt that I could trust him; and that he would understand me, and believe me.

The session started with his asking me how I had been feeling.

"Muddled," I told him. "Confused. Little by little, it's as though everything is going from me. I can barely read or write any more; I can't even help my granddaughter with her Lego. Everything seems to dart around in front of me. And I can't find things-then I find them somewhere completely different. It doesn't make any sense."

All this was spoken in a passionate rush of words. I so wanted him to comprehend what I was going through. I wanted him to cure me of this intruder that was taking over me. I told him about Terry Pratchett's television documentary.

"I might be crazy, but I think I have what he had."

"You're not crazy," he reassured me. "And yes, it is quite possible that you do, indeed, have the same as him. First, however, I should like to run through a few tests."

The following is a list of some of the tests: drawing a clock face came first. It was almost impossible; I couldn't picture what a clock looked like or the order of numbers. Next came drawing squares and circles, and these proved even harder. I then had to remember an address and, gratifyingly, this proved to be quite easy. Then he asked me to draw whatever I wished. I thought for a moment, and decided on a horse. I had always loved drawing horses, and had sold some of my horse drawings. This, surely, would be easy. He passed me a pencil, and I took it from him confidently and positioned my hand. I hesitated then. I did not know where to begin. I could no longer envisage the horse's anatomy. And my hands trembled as I tried and tried to draw something resembling a horse. I fought back tears.

Thereafter, things progressed quickly. The possibility of a brain tumour meant that I was seen as a matter of urgency. Just three days later, I found myself being helped into a white hospital gown. Then was assisted by the radiographer into the MRI room, where I was carefully positioned on the table. I felt like a slab of meat. I was told that I must remain as still as possible, and was warned that I might feel claustrophobic in the tube like scanner. In point of fact I quickly became used to the strange bangs and shaking. I found it oddly hypnotic, and passed the time writing a poem in my head.

Every 10 minutes the radiologist would call from outside the door, checking on me and to let me know how much longer I would have left. I became aware of music playing softly and at one point I felt myself dozing. Perhaps the worst thing was having to keep still for such a length of time; suddenly I would have the urge to scratch, or cough.

Chris drove us home. I felt disorientated; as though the machine was still reverberating in my brain. He stopped off at a filling station, and got out of the car.

"You filled up earlier," I reminded him.

He waved a hand, casually. "I won't be a tick," he assured me. He returned after a few minutes, a big grin on his face: "Eat your heart out," he said, and brandished the Maltesers in his hand – an extra large pack.

I laughed. "You can be so nice sometimes," I told him, hugging him.

"Only, sometimes?" He queried.

"Always, always," I said fiercely.

A week had passed, and I was once again in the surgeon's consulting room.

He shook my hand with a friendly smile, then gestured me to sit down.

"Well, the good news is that you don't have a brain tumour," he informed me, then paused.

"And the bad news," I questioned him?

"It is as you thought," he confirmed. "You have a rare form of Alzheimer's which affects the back part of the brain. He explained about Posterior Cortical Atrophy in more detail, and I tried to comprehend what he was saying. It was hard to take it all in.

It may sound strange but my first, overwhelming reaction was one of relief. Not joy-of course, I could not say that this was a joyful moment – but the relief of having a diagnosis, after years of mental anguish, was very great indeed.

"I will refer you to an Oxford hospital," the neurologist said. "It will be nearer for you, and you are not allowed to be under two consultants."

He wished me luck.

"Keep in touch he said,
"I would like to know how you get on."

It was all over.

I tottered out, feeling almost drunk.

With the truth came a kind of freedom – almost a euphoria
which was difficult to explain, in light of the truth. I was
terrified, yet calm; fearful of the future, whilst resigned.
In other words, I was one big mess of conflicting emotions.

To begin with, we were quiet on the way home;
each absorbed in our own thoughts.

"I don't know what to think," I said to my husband.
"I don't know what to feel."

"Me neither," he admitted.

"I going to look up everything possible about PCA,"
I told him. "I won't allow this to beat me," I continued.

He felt for my hand; I kissed it, and gently placed it on
the steering wheel again. A thought came to me then;
and I laughed, despite myself.

"What," he queried?

"I won't be the allowed to drive any more," I said.
"Oh God, what a relief that will be.
You can be my handsome chauffeur."

The first person I told was my daughter. I had been
worried about this for some time. I was unsure how
she would receive the news. She is a pragmatic young
woman, and I had prepared her for the possible outcome
in advance; however, as mother and daughter we are

particularly close, and I was not looking forward to imparting the news to her. In the event, she reacted with typical sensitivity, focusing on the positive, whilst not minimising the reality. It must be difficult for her to witness my deterioration, and I am so grateful for her support.

Almost the entirety of the next day was taken up by informing friends and family of my condition. It was not an easy thing to do. I tried to be prosaic: I did not want to be the object of pity; I did not want people to treat me any differently from before, or to regard me in a different manner. I wanted my friends to be at ease with me, to be natural with me, and free with their thoughts and opinions, just as previously; I wanted my friends to laugh with me, and tease me, without embarrassment. I was determined not to be defined by my strange disease. I explained to each and every one, that PCA is different from the more usual form of Alzheimer's in many ways, and that its progression is slow. However, I did also touch on the fact that, given time, the Brain Gremlins would spread into other areas.

To my relief, my friends and family have remained loyal to me; they accept me as I am now. When I fumble for words, as, often I do, I turn it into a game; and they have to guess what the words might be. It is rather like "20 questions".

I think of my late father; I think of him often. He would have been heartbroken to know that the little girl he had used to call mouse, now had Alzheimer's. He had been an emotional man, and at the slightest provocation his eyes would well up. He died nearly 14 years ago, a brilliant, and charismatic businessman, whose repartee was legendary. We were both strong characters, and many were our quarrels. He would phone me with the opening words, that I dreaded hearing:

"I've had a fantastic idea," he would commence, in an excited tone; and my heart would sink. I knew that it would lead to one of our arguments. Oh, but how I adored him. Above all, he cared about his family and was proud of each of us. A few months before he died, he gathered my brother, myself, and my mother, together. He told us that he had something important to discuss with us. My mother was holding his hand, I recall. She had already been diagnosed with Parkinson's and dementia.

"I wanted to ask something very important of you," he began, turning to Adrian and myself, in turn.

"You know I have not been well recently." He stopped, cleared his throat, and continued. "If I became very bad, I would not want to continue; I would not want to lose my dignity; more than anything, I would hate that to be the case. Would either of you be prepared to accompany me to Switzerland?" His expression did not waver as he spoke and my mother squeezed his hand.

My brother's face was aghast. "I couldn't," he said, "not in a million years," while shaking his head vehemently.

I stared at my father, trying to process the immensity of what he was requesting. I loved him too much not to agree to his wishes.
In the event, my father died 10 months after that conversation, peacefully, and in his own home. I had had

a premonition that I would not see him again. But, there is an extraordinary appendage to this tale: I had finally settled my poor mother in bed. My father's body had been taken away, and my daughter and niece had arrived. We sat together in the cosy breakfast room and reminisced together, weeping and hugging each other, like lost birds. We continued to reminisce -things he had said, or done; places we had been to, holidays we had shared. I then decided to tell them of my father's request that he had made six months earlier. Wiping away my tears, I explained what my father had requested.

"He wanted to die with dignity," I told my daughter and my niece. "Above all, that was his desire."

It happened then: as I spoke, the lights flickered, on off, on off, on off and then, on again.

Rooted to our seats, the three of us were unable to move. It was quite extraordinary, and how you would be able to explain this phenomenon, I really do not know.

TEN – NO SHAME

The very word "Alzheimer's" is accompanied by a kind of stigma. People have a tendency to recoil in fear and revulsion, in their ignorance. It is spoken about in hushed tones, and with dread. Sometimes, I myself am guilty of avoiding using the word. If I meet someone for the first time, I simply say that I am visually impaired. It is not a lie, nonetheless, it is not quite the truth either. I am not proud of myself for this omission; there should be no shame in having Alzheimer's, yet, instinctively, I shy away from it.

Reflecting back on those difficult, bewildering years prior to diagnosis, I don't know how I kept going; at least now I would be able to enlist help. Pride, however, has a habit of intruding. I remember a particular incident: it was a few weeks after my diagnosis. I was going to visit my daughter in London, and Chris had deposited me at my nearby train station. I was running late and had only just made the train; I clambered into the carriage. The train was packed and I cast about for an empty seat. The only one that was available faced backwards and I found myself dithering, unable to work out how to position myself, but was too proud to ask. I circled round and round, like a dog trying to settle itself; but I just could not work out how to get into the empty seat. Everyone in the carriage was staring at me and I felt so humiliated, so embarrassed. There was nothing for it: in my most dignified tone I addressed my little audience: "I so sorry," I said, "I have a visual impairment, and I am unable to see which is my seat." I could see the relief in their faces: they were not sitting next to a mad woman after all! Several people sprung up to help me, and could not have been kinder. Quite soon after this episode I took to using a white stick. I will never forget that day and cringe, remembering it.

A RANDOM JOTTING

I must have been six or seven – no more.
God existed, and I believed him.

I was small for my age and of a nervous disposition.
I played at being an orphan, and cried myself to sleep.
I remember feeling lonely but don't know why. In the
park one day, I watched two other girls of a similar age,
swinging back and forth. I offered one of them my last
sweet. She looked so confident and I envied her, and
I wanted to be like her; though I had never met her before.
I asked her if she would be my best friend. She declined
both. I dare say that she thought me a little odd.
She would not have been wrong. I think I have always
been a little eccentric, according to my friends.

My parents were very sociable, and went out a lot.
I remember my mother kissing me good night; I remember
the intoxicating smell of her perfume and how beautiful
she looked. I clung to her, because I hated being left with
the childminder; and although my brother was in the room
next to mine, he regarded me as fair bait, and so was no
comfort. The house creaked and felt unfriendly. After my
parents had gone, dutifully, I said my prayers. This was
more complicated than one would have imagined.
My prayers were long and very drawn out. This was due
to my terror of the many disasters which I envisaged
befalling me.

Here is a sample...

Dear God. I hope you are very well and happy. Please look after mummy and daddy and Peter the dog. Please make Adrian stop teasing me. Please don't let there be earthquakes or hurricanes or tornadoes or floods or volcanoes or fires. Or any nasty people and please may mummy and daddy live forever. Please may I live for ever too.

Now, this sounds all very well, having covered everything I could possibly think of, and I would fall asleep immediately; however, I would wake up in the night, and realise that I had forgotten to say Amen. This meant that I would have to repeat the whole process all over again. I recall trying desperately not to fall asleep for a third time.

I remember all this as though it were yesterday.

ELEVEN – COMING TO TERMS

Now, looking back, I realise there was a bona fide reason for my behaviour. I can scroll back and more or less establish how long I have had PCA. Taking into account the years that I had been driving when I was unfit to do so, and also taking into account that my mother had still been alive during that period, I realise that I must have been living with PCA for at least 10 years before I was diagnosed.

People assume that if you have Alzheimer's, you are likely to be in your 80s; I was I was in my late 50s when the Brain Gremlins started their fun and games. There is no cure for Alzheimer's. It is a degenerative disease, and the jury is out as far as available treatments are concerned. At best the tablets might slow things down.

Just in case, however, for three years I dutifully took a drug called Donepezil; I was not aware of any ill effects and so, continued with the drug. However, for several years, I had been plagued by dreadful nightmares. I would be walking endlessly without being noticed or acknowledged; I would be lost in a lonely, urban landscape, and scurrying figures would brush past me as though I did not exist. People who I had loved, were dead; I had killed somebody and was trying to hide the body; in my dream, I would be searching for Chris but he was nowhere to be found. In another dream everyone was laughing at me. The nightmares became increasingly distressing, and destroyed my sleep pattern. It was by chance, when I was having a routine consultation with my neurologist, that she had asked me whether I slept well at night. I told her about the nightmares. Simultaneously, a thought hit me:

"Could it be anything to do with the drug?" I asked her.

"It could be," she confirmed. She explained that this was, indeed, a fairly common side effect. She suggested I take the medication during the daytime instead of at night, but I was unwilling to do so. Since then, I have taken no medication, and the nightmares have ceased.

My brain continued to trundle along at its own pace. Somehow or other, little by painful little, my novel, *The Lupo Stick*, was almost finished. As yet, I did not know whether my heroine would live or die; and then it came to me: I had the perfect ending. After nearly eight years and many shed tears, my novel was finally finished. Having lived with my characters for so long, and under such duress, I felt a mixture of relief and euphoria. I felt, too, a sense of grief – as though I had been bereaved. I wandered around the house, not knowing how to fill my time. My protagonist, Graziella, had dwelt inside me like a twin sister.

Originally I had intended to approach a publisher for *The Lupo Stick*; but then, had a change of heart. *The Lupo Stick* meant so much to me; it represented heartache, love, and loss. How would anyone ever be able to understand what it was like to write a novel when the words danced away from you, and your eyes flitted about, and you could not even read back what you had written? This would be my book, and mine alone. As such, I would self-publish, using one of my own paintings for the cover.

And now, here I am again, writing this;
and it is like déjà vu, as I falter for words,
and my poor husband has to correct the errors.

TWELVE – COPING

In the early days, after my diagnosis, I found a grim kind of fascination in charting my own deterioration. I recall thinking that sometimes I felt so normal that my PCA was a hoax, if anything, I felt freer, in charge of my own body, and able to laugh at myself. At this stage I was still travelling to London every fortnight to visit my daughter. I no longer felt apprehensive; the white stick that I now used, said everything. When I asked for help, it was gladly given. I learnt to trust human kindness. However, the months passed, and I became increasingly aware of the changes within me; they were subtle, stealthy, relentless. I liken it to a runaway train.

It was the little things that floored me: not being able to read meant that I was forever eliciting my husband's help. A tin of fruit that I had opened turned out to be baked beans; if I had a headache and wanted to take paracetamol, I would have to check with him first, in case, inadvertently, I might poison myself. If I needed to turn on a switch, I would fumble for it, uselessly, before eventually locating it. The list of what I was unable to do was becoming longer by the day. Laying the table for more three people was a particular challenge and when I attempted to wrap a parcel, I would become entangled with the Sellotape. Cooking was increasingly stressful, if not downright dangerous. I joked with Chris that he would have to be my sous chef; but inwardly this discussion saddened me greatly, as I had always enjoyed cooking.

Frustrated, despondent, I sat down and wrote an article for the Saturday Times magazine. This was the beginning of another stage for me. I told myself that if I was to be saddled with this wretched disease, the least I could do would be to make people aware of it, and by so doing, I might be able to help others.

In the past I had written many articles for *The Oxford Times Limited Edition Magazine*. These were all about local people of interest. I had also written a regular column on how to write a novel. However, I had never written about myself. Why would I?

I used to belong to a well-known writing group in Oxford; we were all published authors, we would meet every month to discuss how our work was progressing - or not, as the case may be. The venue would be in a pub, sometimes in a member's home, and often we would have a speaker. I loved those meetings; I loved feeling part of something; I loved the camaraderie and the feeling of belonging; I felt faintly bohemian. I was proud that, when asked how many books I had published, I could answer, eleven novels.

Looking back, I think that period was one of the happiest in my life. I had never felt so free as then. Life was an adventure. And now, instead of writing about others' lives, I find myself writing about someone that I no longer recognise, someone timid, and unsteady on her feet, who fumbles for elusive words that will never be found again.

I am jealous of my past; and of my old self.
I shall write about it and shall see where it takes me.

It is a murky winter's day; I am joined on the sofa by my dog and I reflect back on another memory.

I had received an email from Hillary Evans, of Alzheimer's Research UK, requesting that we meet. As a result of this, I was invited to attend an event at the House of Lords, focusing on the subject of Alzheimer's. I was, of course, flattered by this invitation, but nonetheless the prospect of this terrified me, and I was worried days ahead.

Just as we were approaching the House of Lords we found ourselves caught up in a political demonstration, concerning cuts in education; there must have been at least three or four hundred protesters, and the noise was immense. This only served to make me more nervous than I already was, and I shrank into myself, feeling vulnerable. In that moment I wanted nothing more than to be back home, safe in our thatched cottage in Oxfordshire.

We were hustled in by a tense looking security official, then escorted along a series of corridors, and finally into the brightly lit lecture room, where we were made welcome, with canapés and wine. In my head, I repeated my speech over and over again; because of my inability to read, I had memorised it by heart; but suddenly my mind went totally blank. Various people came up to me and introduced themselves and I could feel myself relaxing.
"You have something important to say.
You can do this," I told myself.

We were three speakers in all. I was second.

"Good evening everyone, it is a pleasure to see you all,"
I began. "Now, I'd like you to picture the following…"
And as I spoke, miraculously, my nervousness melted away; I felt empowered and in control, everyone's eyes were pinned

on me, and I felt proud; and yes I did have something to say.I spoke for nearly half an hour. There must have been at least a hundred people in the room, and after the applause had died down, I found myself surrounded. The kind remarks and sincerity were humbling, and rang in my ears all the way back home, in the car.

From that beginning came many other requests, and I found myself in demand as a speaker. These included breakfast television, schools, talks alongside scientists, and an invitation to Women of The World, universities, and numerous other engagements. I then had the idea of arranging a singalong, in our own village. People were so generous. It was winter, and that day was bitterly cold, but despite the bleak weather, the turnout was fantastic, and we raised more than £1000 for Alzheimer's Research UK. That all seems a long time ago, and the Covid pandemic has taken up the mantle now. In addition, my PCA has taken a turn for the worse and I think it unlikely that I would be able to continue speaking in public. My speech is no longer fluent, and I feel self-conscious. Perhaps my audience would feel uncomfortable. I tell myself that everything must have its time.

I count myself fortunate that, although I can no longer read music, or play Chopin, I have discovered the freedom of improvising. I go to the piano, rest my fingers on the keyboard, close my eyes, and let my hands take me wherever they wish to go. The result can be surprisingly successful, and I can while away hours thus. Chris would like me to record my efforts, but that would spoil it for me.

THIRTEEN – SINGING

Earlier on, I talked about my choir, and my sorrow when I realized I would have to abandon it. However, in retrospect, perhaps it was no bad thing, as it has allowed me time to focus on my own singing.

I have this clear memory of myself as a four year-old child. As a treat, my parents had taken me to the London Palladium: the show was almost finished, when the compère asked if any children would like to come up onto the stage and sing. My hand shot up immediately; and there was little me, suddenly on the stage; no nerves in those days. The song that I chose was *How Much is that Doggie in the Window*, and I can still remember the delighted laughter as I sang the woof woof's at the end of each verse.

I have, for as long as I can remember, always sung. My father used to get me to sing to his friends. It must have been very tedious for them. I had singing lessons from the age of nine and I passed all the Royal Academy of Music exams up to Grade 8, with distinction: this was as far as one could go prior to music college. I had hoped to make singing my career, however, my parents had wanted me to go to Switzerland for a year, to 'round off my education'. I did not want to go, and my brother backed me up in this; however, my parents were adamant and, with reluctance, off I went.

To begin with things were better than I had expected, but after a few weeks, the bullying began and I lost all my confidence. In addition, I was ill with severe anaemia for

much of the time there and was deeply unhappy.
When I returned home to England, I was so lacking in
confidence that I flunked my audition for my entry to
the Royal College of Music. I was devastated for nearly
a year. I wanted nothing more to do with singing.
I did some modelling, then went into my father's wine
business. And at the age of just 20, I married my first
husband, Irving. I was too young and naive to marry;
and we divorced a few years later; however, we
remained the best of friends, and the result is my
lovely daughter and granddaughter.

I had a lapse of about two years, without singing.
Then, a chance meeting with a renowned German
singing teacher restored my confidence. I remained
with him for eight years, however, he was an alcoholic
and drank his way steadily throughout the morning, until
he was barely coherent, and the brandy bottle was empty.
When I moved to Oxfordshire it meant that I had to find
a new singing teacher, and, inevitably, we lost touch.

A series of teachers then followed, none of whom were
quite right for me, and, on a whim, I contacted my old
tutor. His wife answered the phone. He had died,
she told me. He had fallen down the stairs.

"Oh, I am so sorry," I said, close to tears.

"He used to think very highly of you," she said,
then added, "but you know what he was like."

I nodded, and imagined him, drunk,
falling down the steep staircase of his three-storey house.

I have been with my current teacher now, for 12 years. A renowned opera singer, Geoff also teaches and adjudicates at the Royal College of Music. I have so much to thank him for; despite my illness, and despite the passage of time, my voice is better than it has been for many years. I would be lost without his help and encouragement, and I always come away from my lessons inspired and elated.

If I had one piece of advice regarding Alzheimer's, it would be to sing your heart out, every day. Do not worry about forgetting the words: just sing la, la, la; take a deep breath, forget your inhibitions and sing like there is no tomorrow.

FOURTEEN – CORONAVIRUS

I should begin this by saying how very fortunate I am.
I live in a beautiful thatched cottage, set in a rural
location, surrounded by trees, nature, and lovely walks.
However, one always feels vulnerable and one is never
quite free of the possibility that you will be next. The
hangman is never far away, hovering above; a grim
spectre, lying in wait, determined to trash our beautiful
idyll. I think if we are honest, most of us are living with
a constant dread. Chris and I are so close that we live
in terror of one of us being without the other. It never
quite abates. It is a lottery; how would I live without my
Christopher? It is simply unthinkable; and so we don't
think, and every precious day is a tick in the box.

And while I ponder on the might have been,
and the will be, and the maybe; and while I fret
about not being able to buy Arborio rice to make
risotto, others shiver in their cardboard beds and
hold out plaintive hands that have become chafed
with the bitter cold, and only the dogs get fed.

So, you see: I have no right to complain.
Here is a poem of mine that reflects something I saw.

WHO CARES

A young man and his dog.
Isolated figures, etched in black ink.
Who notices them, there, poised on the brink?
Who notices the small dog,
or the young man with the blank, glazed eyes?
What dark, tortured thoughts
pester and fester and plague him?
Impervious to them, as they are to him,
He gazes down from the beckoning bridge.
Heedless of the meaningless, merciless roar of traffic -
Motto perpetuoso -
He hears only the demons of his soul.
Two silhouettes trust tightly together.

Trusting little dog wagging its stubby tail.
Big Ben striking 5 o'clock;
and in perfect synchronisation
the young man raises his arms.

Two silhouettes flying through the air,
somersaulting, twirling;
and traffic grinds to a screaming halt,
as at last they are noticed.

How has it happened, this sad ending?
Crushed ambitions, hopes thwarted;
So young, unloved son.

Oh, and poor, small dog,
who had no say in the matter.

FIFTEEN – FACING REALITY

I feel as though my life is a race against time. In part, it could be because of Covid 19. But, there is another reason. I have always told myself that I am not old; the word did not apply to me. My refusal to concede to it was, I suppose, vanity, and a hankering for the past. And I am ashamed to admit this. "Vanity of vanities, all is vanity; except the pure soul." But there is a reason today, for my morose mood: spurred on by the Coronavirus, Chris and I tentatively broached the prickly subject of Carers. Not for now, he hastily told me, but just in case, in years to come.

I was taken aback to say the least. I could feel myself blanching. In truth, I had been worrying about the future for some time, then pushed it aside. In fact, thinking about it, it had been at the back of my mind for longer than I had realised, and I kept thrusting it to one side. It was like an intrusive, ticking clock. And because neither of us had spoken of the subject, it had become unmentionable.

And now, with Chris sitting beside me,
he maps out my future.

"This is grim," I say.

"Yes," he agrees, squeezing my hand, "but necessary." And he returns to filling in the endless form with all the personal details, which constitute my life. He is being pragmatic, as he always is, and I cannot blame him, for confronting the truth, but nonetheless, it hurts.

I want to rage at time passing, and to protest that this is a mistake, and that I am still young; but it would be a lie, wouldn't it?

I go into the garden, because I think I might cry. Appropriately, it has been raining for most of the day; but the rain is gentle and the dripping leaves are green, orange, and topaz. And on the bird table, a green finch feasts. My mood lifts as I watch Elgar circling the garden, chasing pigeons, poor things, and barking with excitement.

It is, after all, I tell myself, only precautionary.

SIXTEEN – PRISON

"It's like being in prison."

I caught the tail end of the woman's conversation
as she passed by in the street. It was a tantalising snippet
to overhear, and I have often wondered about it.
The well-dressed woman's remark took me back fifteen
years. For five years, once a week, I had taught creative
writing in a High Security men's prison; one thing is for
certain: she had clearly never seen the inside of a prison.

I remember my first, nervous day there, being frisked
for security and relinquishing my phone. I had been
told in advance not to wear provocative clothing, and
on no account must I divulge my surname. I was then
accompanied to the education area, thence to the room
which had been allotted to me. I was shown where the
emergency panic button was located and attempted to
look relaxed. My mouth felt dry. Just be yourself, I thought.

I had prepared the morning's lesson ahead, just as
I would my regular adult education class. The room was
laid out like any other classroom, and above the entrance
a sign read, "Creative Writing." The first two students
poked their heads round the door, then did a double
take when they saw me. The older of the two gave
a low wolf whistle when he saw me.

"What's creative writing, Miss? He demanded.

"You'll have to come in and find out for yourself,"
I said lightly.

He laughed, then narrowed his eyes,
as though assessing me.

"I suppose I have nothing to lose," he said.

"Except for your virginity,"
his colleague quipped, and they sauntered in.

"I shall ignore that," I countered,
as the two men giggled and sat down, expectantly.

One by one the other men trickled in, intrigued to see
a new face, and a woman's, at that. As expected, they were
keen to show off. There were nine of them in total that first
day, but I knew that would vary, depending on newcomers.
They were a mixed bunch as regards ethnicity, and their
ages ranged from about 20 to 55. I introduced myself by
saying that I was a published novelist, then explained
what creative writing involved.

I had their attention now. "First things first," I told them.
"Creative writing is all about expressing yourself in words
and in feelings. It doesn't matter if you are hopeless at
grammar, or if you can't spell; it's about committing pen
to paper in a way that makes you feel good about yourself.
It is about telling stories, and the pleasure you derive from
doing so."

By now all eyes were on me - with the exception of one
young lad, who cut in loudly, "Boring, boring."

For a brief moment I was taken aback, then I recovered my equilibrium. "You don't have to stay if you don't want to," I said with a friendly smile. He did not leave, however, and the other men glared at him.

I gave them a preliminary exercise to do: "Imagine you are fearful of something. What is it? I would like you to really think about this and for you to describe your feelings."

I listened to the scratching of pens, the sighs of concentration and the sounds of rubbings out. From time to time they would look up pensively as though searching for inspiration, before resuming again. Except for the Joker in the room, who was pulling faces at everyone, you could have heard a pin drop as they wrote for half an hour.

I asked each of the men in turn to read their piece out loud. As expected, there was resistance at this: "I couldn't, Miss... Oh, it's crap... Oh, it's shit... I don't want anyone to see it."

These were some of the protestations.

"But you can, I promise you can.
Just be truthful with what you have written."

I won the battle; the results were surprising; there was some really good writing amongst them; in some cases sensitive, while others were full of resentment. At all times, their writing was heartfelt.

I felt privileged that they had trusted me enough to confide in me. One of the men said, "Good on you, Miss," and I felt a lump in my throat.

"See you next week," I said.

The week had gone by, during which time I'd had an idea. I had noticed that displayed around the public rooms were paintings produced by the inmates; it occurred to me that we could do the same with my class. The best stories would be displayed on a noticeboard for two weeks, giving everyone a chance to read what had been written. My idea had been approved by the head of education, and that day I put it to the men themselves.

"What do you think?" I asked. "Do you like the idea?"

With the exception of the troublemaker from the week before, they were all enthusiastic. I had realised by then that he suffered from ADHD.

"You don't know what it's like being in here, Miss," he burst out suddenly.

I had already planned the programme for the day, however, his passionate words stunned me. I stared at him.

"Then you can tell me," I told him. We're going to make this into a poem, starting with the words "you don't know what it's like being in here", and you can write the first line while I chalk it up, on the board."

We went round the room, fired up with a new energy. It took up the whole of the lesson, and we were all exuberant.

"Well this is definitely one to go on the wall," I told them.

I remember one particular day. The theme I had set for the class was, happiness, and everyone was quietly beavering away -that is, except two young lads who were comparatively new to the class. It was obvious, from their giggling, that they were up to something. I pretended to take no notice; it did not take a genius to guess what they were up to. I waited for the other students to finish what they had written; then it was the turn of the new boys. They shuffled to their feet, still giggling.

As expected, what they had written contained every smutty word in the dictionary. It was now my turn to have some fun. I put on a serious expression and started to analyse what they had written, correcting their grammar as I went. Systematically, I went through the writing, correcting and commenting, all the while, trying to keep a straight face. By now the two of them were squirming in their seats and everybody was laughing; I could almost feel sorry for them.

Very quietly I then said, "What you wrote wasn't clever or funny." I stared hard at each of them in turn. "If you disrespect me like that again, I'm afraid that you won't be welcome in the class again, which would be a great shame as you are both good writers.

Teaching in prison gave me an insight into another world
and I hope, and I like to believe, that I was able to do
some good, in return for what they gave to me.

As I got to know the men, with all their quirks, I felt
emboldened, and gave them topics to write which
stretched their imagination.

I remember one particular day at the prison; all was quiet,
and I was doing the rounds, offering help to those who
needed it. One boy in particular needed assistance;
he was of a surly disposition and spoke little; but he was
a diligent worker. That day he was in a petulant mood.

"Miss, I need a folder to put my work in," he demanded.

It was a reasonable request, but rules meant that
I was not allowed to use the stationery – heaven knows
why. I explained this to him, and his eyes darkened.

"That's not fair. I need one," he said.

"I know it's not fair, and I've just remembered I've got a
spare one at home, that you can keep," I told him.

Three weeks passed, but he did not turn up.
Each week I had brought with me the folder, in case.
And then, on the fourth week, he appeared.

"Hi," I said casually, as if there had been no interlude.
"I've got that folder that you wanted,"
and I presented it to him.

He stared at me in astonishment.
"You remembered," he said.

"Of course," I replied.

"They banned me from education", he explained.
Thereafter he was always being banned, but he never
missed a quick hello, to me, from the door.

Then, after a few months I had an idea. The more I
thought about it, the more excited I became: why not
start a magazine for them? I liaised with the computer
class in order to do so, and the result was a triumph.

There are so many more stories that I could recount about
my time teaching in prison; but I shall finish with a remark,
made by one of the inmates. He was a big, taciturn man,
whose silence made him seem menacing. That day he was
even more silent than usual; his eyes seemed to be boring
into me, and I felt discomfited.

Then he spoke. "You're different from the other teachers,
Miss," he said and paused for a moment,
so that I wondered what would follow next.
What he said astounded me.

"You inspire us," he went on. "If we'd had teachers like you
at school, we wouldn't be in here."

I'll never forget his words, and I felt so very proud,
and by the same token, so very sad, and humbled.

SEVENTEEN – CHANGES

Memories are so arbitrary, aren't they? For no reason at all a thought will suddenly come into my head.

I hate technology. Quite simply, it terrifies me. I would love to return to the days of typewriters and Tippex. Better still, I would like to cherish the sensation of pen and ink, and my excited fingers would fly faster and faster, barely able to keep up with my inspiration. However, it is technology which allows me to continue to write, albeit with much swearing. In order to write this, Chris sits at my side, and I dictate to him. For this, I use Siri on my iPhone. We continue until I have written a respectable number of words, then transfer it to Dragon. This is the name of the voice recognition software I use; however, Dragon is prone to making outlandish gaffs. Just now, it interpreted the word "gaff" as "death"! Between us, we muddle through and what should take minutes, takes hours. Poor Chris. I joke that he is the sacrificial lamb; but really it is no joke.

We made a list today; it chronicled the changes which have taken place in the last months.

The well-known advert for Specsavers could certainly apply to my own experiences. The other day I had a fascinating conversation with my rug, mistaking it for my dog. Later that same day I could not find my hat anywhere and went in search. Eventually I found it. I was actually wearing it. I had no recollection of having put the hat on.

I potter round the cottage slowly nowadays, unsure what it is that I am looking for, remembering what it was for a second then forgetting it again. The Brain Gremlins have decided to travel further afield. They are adventurous nowadays and their journey has taken them to pastures new. I gaze around my own sitting room for a clue, not recognising it. A sea of blankness envelops me. What am I supposed to be doing? I know where I am; I can talk; but my mind is an empty blank, everything is out of focus. I sigh deeply. With that sigh comes recognition and rationality.

We are about to go for a walk. It is that simple, you would think. I put on my lipstick and eyeliner; go downstairs.

Chris looks at me gently. "You've got black eyeliner on around your lips," he tells me.

I rub my lips fiercely to get rid of it, succeeding in making it look ghoulish. This is happening increasingly, nowadays, as colours play tricks on me. And I have to consult Chris just in case I walk outside looking like Dracula.

My speech has taken a turn for the worse. More, and more, I flounder for words. I love words, I love the innuendos and subtleties, but more often than not, they allude me. I cannot retain words now; anything more than three or four seconds, then they slither away, never to be resurrected.

Reading back what I have just written, I confront myself – that self who is me. I take stock of this person who lives inside me. Do I expect too much of her? Or perhaps, too little? As my words fail me, I could grieve for them, or I could accept what is in store for me. Perhaps the trouble with me is that I think too much; I analyse too much. As Paul McCartney would say, "Let it be, let it be."

I glance through the window; the sun glares through.
How lush is its orange tint. And I don a thick jacket and
go into the garden. The days are getting longer, and today,
a kind friend presented me with a bunch of early daffodils.
My husband put them in a jug. I used to love arranging
flowers, but I become muddled now and he has taken
on the role of florist.

I walk around the perimeter of the garden, slowly,
so as not to fall - the garden is large and irregular.
One day I shall get round to having it levelled,
in order to make it less of a hazard.

Our garden abuts a large field, close to the village pond,
and Chris joins me there. All at once, we see a grey
squirrel; it stops in its tracks, as though in bewilderment.
It now faces a tricky dilemma: the water is high, following
recent rain, but the squirrel is determined to reach the
other side of the bank. We watch it with bated breath,
to see what it will do next. The creature stares at us for
several moments, then does something extraordinary.
It plunges into the water and swims to safety, its little
feet paddling frantically.

We watch him climb up the opposite bank, bedraggled
but victorious. It was one of life's special moments.
We turn to each other. I feel a wave of emotion.

"I have an idea, Darling. I would like to interview you."
I say, with a firmness I do not feel.

He looks at me askance. Already, I can sense his resistance.

"What are you talking about," he asked, with a frown.

"I want to remember this moment for ever." I explain.
"I want your true feelings and to know what you are
thinking. I need to know what your feelings are towards
me; have they altered? I want to know what changes
you have noticed about me. You must be honest."

"I've noticed how much more anxious you have become
about everything. Also, you seem to want everything
done immediately."

I see you looking around things around the house.
You take an age to find what it is you are after.
Sometimes you ask if you are upstairs or downstairs.

You are unsteady on your feet now, and in particular,
coming down the stairs is a problem.

Whilst you can still hold a conversation, I see it is very
difficult, and sometimes I have to prompt you for words.

EIGHTEEN – LOVE

Today is Valentine's Day, and I forgot. Two reasons:
the first, because nowadays I forget everything and, the
second, there is little to celebrate. Because of lockdown,
Chris has been unable to find an appropriate card, so he
has adapted one that says happy birthday, instead. Here
is what he wrote: "We cannot celebrate, but we have each
other, that is all that matters.. With all my love, Chris."
He has written the message in beautiful calligraphy.

I felt terrible that I had forgotten. I wish I could have
made a card for him, but it would have been illegible.

Chris and I had first met 23 years ago, in a popular pub,
local to both of us. We had much in common
and gravitated towards each other almost instantly.
I loved his gentleness and kindness, his quiet sense of
humour and his sensitivity. And now I shall embarrass
him by saying that he was also tall and handsome.
We went out for about a year, however, he was going
through a stressful time with his work, and we parted
as friends, meeting up occasionally after that and at
this moment, as I write, he comes into the living room.

"I am writing about you," I tell him.
"So you had better be nice to me."

He pulls a gargoyle face at me, and I laugh.
I am so very lucky. He is truly my love. And now I can
hear him practising the guitar. He is nothing, if not
persistent. He dreams of being another Eric Clapton.

"I'm going to talk about Richard, would you mind?"
I ask Chris.

"Of course not," he says.

"You won't be hurt in any way will you?"

"Of course not," he says again.

"You know how much I love you," I tell him, and he nods.

And so to Richard.

I met Richard during the period that Chris and I were just friends. A big bear of a man with a beard to match, if I had one word to describe him it would be charismatic. His quick wit and his soft voice drew everyone to him, and I can still hear his wicked chuckle. He was a principled man, and would judge somebody by whether or not he would want to share a trench with them. Richard was wonderfully eccentric; he loved little gadgets and antiques, and collecting strange objects. He loved fine food and fine wine, playing tricks on people, and doing crosswords and puzzles. He loved fishing for his own supper, and drawing cartoons, and I could go on and on. But he did not go on. We had nearly 5 years together but then came that terrible day. It was night-time; earlier he had told me that he couldn't imagine life without me. How prescient was his remark. Only minutes later, I turned to him; his face was a puce red, and his head was rotating around and around. I knew straightaway that he was having a heart attack. I waited for the ambulance to arrive; it seemed to take forever. I could not save him.

It was inevitable that Chris and I would get together again; he had always been there. Our love is so deep--even our dog regards us as a single entity, one without the other would not work. But I shall always remember Richard and be sad: he died too young. And sometimes I have a horrible nightmare in which both Richard and Chris are alive and I have to choose between them.

There are so many different ways of love and loving, and mine embraces every kind; and in three months' time, Chris and I will be celebrating our twelfth wedding anniversary. I have no regrets.

NINETEEN – SHIVERING WINTER

It is a freezing, sub-zero day; the sort of day that could tempt you into remaining in bed, only to surface for some sustenance. It necessitates layer upon layer of woolly clothing. Getting dressed involves much planning ahead nowadays and even more patience--which does not come naturally to me. Oh, what a muddle. The multi-layers include the following: two camisoles, one polo-neck jumper, a tunic, double thick, and socks. Oh – and some very unsexy knickers. All these items have the potential to throw me into a tizz: inside out polo necks; back to front tunics; odd socks. And, did I put on a camisole on or not, and which way up is the item supposed to be? I end up with frayed nerves, fit to scream with frustration. I hate the whole rigmarole of getting dressed in the morning; it takes forever. Oh bring back summer and skimpy dresses!
In the end, after numerous failures, I have to resort to Chris, yet again. Poor man.

I used to be so quick at doing things and I did it without thought. I am jealous of who I was; I try not to think of who I will become, and because my cognitive function is largely unimpaired, I find that I am observing my own deterioration. I feel sad for my husband and sad for my daughter and sad for my granddaughter. PCA strips you of your dignity and, as the years go by, you become less and less capable of doing things for yourself. But I am soldiering on. I shall put on my happy face instead, and tell myself how bloody lucky I am. And I am, I am. It's just that sometimes things get to me.

This morning we brave the weather and go on to the nature reserve, both of us trussed up like an oven-ready turkey. I had wanted to go on my own, with the dog, but Chris no longer allows me to walk by myself in case I fall. Many are the disagreements we have had about this.

"You can't stop me," I tell him.

"Yes I can," he says. "I can follow you."

"Really, you can be exasperating, you know."

"I'm right," he says.

"You can't stop me," I say.

"Yes I can. I can walk 10 yards behind you.
How does that sound?"

And, of course, I laugh: he is so caring. I vow to myself that when the weather is better I shall trick him somehow and walk on my own, with Elgar. We are very late this morning, because I wanted to work on my book – if that is what it turns out to be. Anyway... I could not find my reading glasses anywhere, despite extensive searching. Eventually I discovered them in the soap dish; goodness knows how they ended up there. Half the morning has, by now, been wasted and Chris, who has three antique clocks in his study, understandably, is becoming tetchy.

We walk to the nature reserve; it is deserted, which comes as no surprise; four days of relentless rain has reduced the area to a quagmire. In addition, ice has formed, making it perilous. The dog trots along between us; I am sure that he thinks we are a single entity; he loves each of us equally.

I cling onto Chris; my feet crunch on the frozen ice. There is a slight gradient up to the kissing gate and I slither onto it and grab Chris's arm to prevent me from ending up in the mud. The white ice is menacing and beautiful. Elgar tests the ground gingerly, breaking pieces of ice as he does so. He decides that he is safe after all, and starts to play whole heartedly. Everything is a game for him. Then, all at once, we spot an unusual large white bird, disturbed by our presence. It flies away, white on white, and we realise it was a large egret; it is only the second time I have seen one and I feel privileged. Nobody else is about; there is just us and nature, and Elgar, who is now playing with a stick that is bigger than himself.

Back home, in the warmth, we make a start on supper. I used to love to cook, but nowadays I enlist the help of my sous chef; without him I am apt to be rather dangerous. I resented his presence at first; cooking used to be my territory; now I find that I rather like it; it feels homely, companionable – though I must admit we have a few differences of opinion.

A RANDOM JOTTING

LET'S TALK ABOUT THE WEATHER

Have you noticed there are definite rules when it comes to going for a walk? The different types of people you will encounter make for a variety of conversations and you need to adjust your facial expressions accordingly, in order not to appear rude. It is, therefore, fraught with possible misunderstandings, and you have to be something of a psychologist in order to switch from one mode to another. You need to be able to pin a smile on your face at a moment's notice.

So let's start with the weather. Here are some obvious openers. Here are some typical offerings you might hear on your travels: morning, lovely day isn't it; good morning, not very nice is it; a bit brighter than yesterday, isn't it? Chatty people might be more adventurous: "It's like Siberia, isn't it?" This will be accompanied by shivering for good measure. "Looks like rain, doesn't it?" They might say, looking up at the sky. Then there is Mr Glum. Mr Glum has no intention of speaking to anybody. A grunt is all he can muster in reply to whoever has dared to speak to him. Mr Hearty is just as bad but in the opposite way: his heartiness is annoying beyond belief. The various permutations are endless. There has to be a remark of some kind. When on a walk, you should never pass anyone without some acknowledgement; it is plain rude. The correct etiquette at all times should be adhered to.

Dogs are a useful accessory, of course: they can do the talking for you; example: oh, what a lovely dog; oh, how sweet he is; how old is it; Is it a boy or a girl? What breed is it? Is it friendly?

Let's deal with cyclists next. Call me grumpy, but where are your manners? Why aren't you using a bell so that in advance, we know you are about to round the corner at full speed; and unsuspecting pedestrians will end up being pushed into the lane in order to get out of the way. As for runners – they are a silent menace as they zigzag around you, and almost collide with you; and in my case, surely my white stick should alert them, but apparently it doesn't. They have no intention of slowing and are frequently arrogant in the extreme. Maybe I am just envious.

Anyhow, that's enough of my grousing, and I must confess that I was guilty of worse crimes in the not too distant past.

TWENTY – PAINTING

As one of my faculties fails, another takes its place.
I realise that my vision has greatly altered, however, my
ability to recognise people's voices compensates for what
is lacking with my eyes. It is weird: I know what I can see;
I know what I can comprehend. I can fully understand what
people are saying and I contribute without a problem,
to conversations. However, my brain just does not
process the information.

A couple of years ago, my neurologist asked me if I was
colour-blind. This surprised me.

 "No, I told him, why do you ask?"

"Because PCA does tend to cause that to happen,"
 he replied.

And now, here we are, on cue. I have always loved
painting. In the past I have sold several of my pictures,
and I particularly liked to paint horses and dogs; now, I
can no longer do figures and have turned to landscapes
– though I have to ask Chris what the colours are. I can no
longer use acrylic paints because they are too complicated
for me, however, I have discovered the joys of oil pastels.

I could spend hours painting; it is so satisfying, but I am
rather too prolific, and am running out of space. I am
reminded of when my daughter was little, and she would
return home from school with another soggy offering and
a beaming smile. I would then try to decipher what it
was supposed to be.

After writing this chapter, I made a fatal mistake. I tried to draw a horse; it was absolutely impossible for me. I tried and tried again and again, but the strange markings I had made on the paper bore no resemblance to anything. My hands shook, and I felt heartbroken. And now, my mood has gone from optimism to despair. I feel as though I have been kidding myself. I feel helpless and useless; and I want to howl with rage. But still, there is a little bit of me that makes me go on, and this is just one of my moods, and it will pass because it has to.

TWENTY-ONE – A CHANCE MEETING

It was the very beginning of September. The Cornish sea already hinted at autumn. Once, it would have tempted me. For a moment I prevaricated; I could imagine myself plunging into it; that moment of icy contact. It was our last day, and instead we went for a warming coffee. From behind me a voice called out my name. I turned; I did not recognise the man, and looked inquiringly at him as he walked towards me. Clearly I looked bewildered, and he explained that he had stayed at my cottage when I was doing B and B.

"How extraordinary," he said. "It must be about 16 years since I last saw you." And he took off his sunglasses. "You haven't changed at all," he said. "This is extraordinary, isn't it? And I agreed that it was; in reality I could not remember him at all. I went through the motions with a wooden smile.

"Yes, what a coincidence indeed."

I felt uncomfortable; did he know about my Alzheimer's? Had he read any of my articles--and why should it matter? We chatted for a few minutes – the usual pleasantries, then we said our goodbyes. I still had no idea who I had been talking to. I can only assume that he had changed beyond recognition. I felt shaken by the encounter.
So long ago, so long ago.

It was 16 years ago. I had just decided that I would do B and B, as I was going through a lean patch with my writing. At this point, both my parents were still alive and my father was horrified by the idea.

"You can't," he told me emphatically.

"I can," I said.

"It could be dangerous," he said. "A woman on her own with strangers. Couldn't you just try it out for a bit?" He queried.

"No," I retorted.

"Why not," he countered?

"You need a bed to do B and B," I reminded him. Trying not to laugh.

"Oh, I forgot about the bed," he confessed, looking crestfallen; and bless him, my father insisted on buying one for me.

The bed duly arrived three days later. It took three strong men, a lot of huffing and puffing, and a hefty tip, to manoeuvre the wretched thing into its new home.

I rang my father to tell him that the bed had arrived, and to thank him.

"I still don't like the thought of you being on your own with these strangers," my father grumbled.

"I'll be fine," I tried to reassure him. "Don't forget I'll have Schubert to keep me company," I continued. Schubert was my then German Shepherd, and was very protective of me.

The first thing I did was to register with the tourist information office, so that my B and B would be listed. Immediately I was inundated with companies wanting to sell me various soaps, shampoos and hand-creams.

And so I prepared the two spare rooms in readiness. They looked fit for royalty.

Now, all I had to do was wait.

The phone call came three days later.

"Is that Vine Cottage?"
The man's voice on the other end of the telephone asked.

"Yes it is," I confirmed. "Can I help you?"

"I'm working in your area and I wondered if you had any vacancies for three nights, in your cottage?" He asked. "It looks lovely, in the picture," he added.

"Yes, yes, it is."

His voice was pleasant, and he had a faint stammer; you can tell a lot by a voice; he did not sound like a murderer.

"I'd like to make a booking, please, if that's alright with you. For tonight."

"Of course," I answered.
"What sort of time would you be arriving?

"About 7 pm," he replied. "Is that okay?"

"Yes, that would be fine," I said, and I took down his details.

"See you later," he said, and rang off."

It was still quite early in the morning. I rushed around in a manic frenzy, fed the horse, the dog and two cats; and then I went upstairs to the bedroom.

I blinked. Closed my eyes, and opened them again. The bedroom was shrouded in a haze; the room appeared to be playing tricks on me. Then I realised that the haze was moving; the whole room was alive, literally alive, with fleas. The two culprits were lying on the bed, luxuriating on a carpet of fleas. I remember screeching in disbelief and flinging off the cats, unceremoniously.

Oh God, oh God, a room full of bloody fleas! And a booking for my first guest, later that same day.

Willing myself to calm down, I clambered into the car and set off to the pet shop, mindful of the sneakily placed speed camera. The pet shop was surprisingly busy for the early hour, and I did my utmost not to show my impatience as I waited my turn. One woman was holding everybody up whilst she debated whether or not to buy a toy dinosaur, or a squeaky snake for her Chihuahua. Eventually it was my turn, and I explained my predicament to the young woman, who looked at me sympathetically.

"I am so sorry, but we are completely out of flea spray," she apologised. "Everybody's got fleas at the moment, and we won't be getting a delivery for several days.

You could try the supermarket," the girl suggested as an afterthought. "They sometimes sell flea spray."

I dashed across the road; but no, they all had fleas as well. This was turning into a farcical nightmare.

"Why not try the vet, that's your best bet,"
the girl at the supermarket offered.

Oh, how silly of me not to think of that.
With renewed hope, I got back into the car and drove to the vet. Please, oh please, I prayed to myself, let God exist. And he must have taken pity on me as two cans were available. I bought them both.

Back home, time was passing at an uncomfortable rate. The one good thing was that the cats were nowhere to be seen.

I have never been one for obeying instructions; I find them excessively boring. Without ado, I stripped the bed and sprayed just about everything in sight, leaving my fingers on the can nozzle. No fleas could possibly survive such an onslaught.

However, I became aware of a strange sensation in my index and middle fingers; it was a tingling sensation and my fingers were becoming more numb by the minute. I peered down at my hands, in disbelief. It had ceased to resemble a finger; instead, there was and black and white blancmange that throbbed with pain. I scrambled into the car once more, and drove as fast as I could, directly to the doctor's. I was able to see him straightaway, as an emergency. He examined my fingers as though they were a rare specimen, with great interest.

"How interesting," he said, and twisted my fingers round and round for good measure. "You have severe frostbite," he concluded. "I have never heard of anyone having frostbite in summer." Cheerfully, he went on to tell me that had I left it for long I would have needed to have the fingers amputated.

I could feel myself blanching in terror.

"Don't worry," he continued. "You'll be fine. May I ask what happened?"

Shame-faced, I told him about the fleas.

He laughed. "Next time, might I suggest that you read the instructions."

I nodded.

I returned home, considerably relieved and armed with medication.

After the stress of the morning, I felt shattered but also relieved. The cats had been newly de-flead, and were still recovering from their ordeal. I set about making the beds. Fortunately I had several pairs of everything. I reinstated all the little touches that were in the room--the shampoo, the soap, the hand cream, the tea and coffee, and the orchid that a friend had recently given to me.
Then I firmly closed the door of the room.

The guest arrived punctually, and was delighted with his room; there was no hint of the morning's shenanigans, although he did comment on the unusual smell. I explained to him that the previous guest had worn a very strong after-shave.

The following day all traces of the fleas had disappeared.

I am vegetarian, and for my guest's breakfast, I cooked scrambled egg, tomatoes, with Worcester sauce, and fried bread. He wrote in my new visitor's book,
Best breakfast I ever had. Thanks for lovely stay.

There are many other stories I could relate from the B and B years. My guests were mostly businessmen, who stayed long-term. I came to know them well, and they were always respectful. I was single at the time, but rarely felt anxious; I had made it clear from the beginning that the B and B did not come with extras. Teaching in prison had seasoned me, and I was used to male banter.

There was one day, however, when a new guest came to stay for the night, and made me feel uneasy. One of the first things he told me was that he owned a golf club. I confess that I don't know much about golf but I do know one thing: if you own a golf club, you are likely to be extremely rich. I could not help noticing that my guest's Ford had seen better days. He smelled of cigarettes and beer. And he asked if I lived on my own. Quickly, I invented a husband who was away lecturing. I let my German Shepherd into the room, who bounded towards him. The man backed away, in surprise.

"Oh, I didn't know you had a dog," he said nervously.
"Is he friendly? "

"Usually," I replied with an enigmatic smile, which I knew
would not reassure him.

I showed him into his room, then left him to it.

He made himself at home and stayed in the bath
for so long that I wondered what he was up to in there.
He emerged finally, nearly an hour later, wearing nothing
but scanty pants and a small hand towel. To say I was
disconcerted would be an understatement. I slept with
my dog in my room that night.

The following morning he came down for breakfast in
a smart dark suit, and sat where one of the cats usually sat.
I made my guest a breakfast of mushrooms on toast; then
noticed the butter was suspiciously smooth. The cat had
been at it again. Inwardly, I repressed a giggle. He had
an important meeting to attend, he told me,
emphasising the word 'important'.

He left quite soon afterwards. He stood up to go.
What he did not realise was that his smart dark suit
was covered with whitish cat fur.

Perhaps I was being unfair about him, but no, I knew the
sort of person he was and I was not sorry for him.

There is one further anecdote about B and B,
which I would like to impart.

It was a hot summer's day. I was just about to set off for a walk with the dog, when the phone rang. Breathlessly, I ran to pick it up before the answer machine kicked in.

"Hello," I said.

"Is that Vine Cottage," enquired a man with a strong Irish accent.

"Yes it is," I told him, putting on my formal voice.

"Ah, well hello there. Would you be doing bed and breakfast, by chance?"

His Irish brogue made me smile.

"Yes, yes, I do."

"Ah, that's grand, and it's a nice day here in Dublin," he said. "What's it like where you are?"

"It's really lovely," I told him, smiling broadly now. This was certainly an unusual opening for a conversation.

"How many days are you thinking of staying?" I asked him.

"I was wanting three nights, beginning from Friday evening," he told me. "How would that be?"

"That would be fine," I told him, trying to imagine what he might look like.

"You sound very nice," he told me.
"Maybe we could share a room."

"I think not," I said." It occurred to me then:
"So what brings you here," I asked him.

"I'm coming over for a wedding," he explained.

I groaned then. "Oh no," I said. By now I felt quite at
home with him and was able to joke – "That means
you'll be coming back in the middle of the night,
rat arsed and singing."

He paused for a moment, "That's not the case," he said,
in a jolly tone: "One, I don't drink, two, I can't sing,
and three, I'm the officiating priest."

When the day itself came, he turned out to be a smallish
man with mischievous eyes. He was quite shy, surprisingly
and he had bought a gift for me – a mug with a horse on
it. We had a fascinating evening, talking about politics and
religion and his job as a priest.

He left early on the Monday and gave me a big hug.
"God bless", he said.

TWENTY-TWO – TIME IS TICKING BY

As I write this I feel as though my life is a race against time. You can kid yourself up to a point, then something else goes wrong, and down you go.

This morning I could not get into the cottage. I was locked out. I could feel a rising panic within me; that hot fear of hopelessness. I tried the key every which way, and it didn't help that my fingers was shaking, like a demented tap dancer. I was on the point of tears. All I wanted was to be able to get in to my own house, was that too much to ask?

Thankfully, minutes later, Chris returned from an appointment. "What's happened," he asked me.

Sobbing, "I couldn't unlock the door," I told him. "I couldn't unlock the fucking door. I'm trapped outside my own home and I couldn't get in or out. What am I supposed to do?" I yelled in frustration. "It's so difficult, everything is so fucking difficult."

Later that day, I went to make myself an instant cappuccino; you could say that I'm addicted to them. I prepared it in readiness then had to answer a quick telephone call. I returned to my cappuccino in anticipation. My cappuccino had gone; how could that be? I could even smell it, close by. And then I spotted it: instead of pouring the mixture into my mug, I had poured it straight onto the floor. I gave a strangulated yelp.

"Well what's wrong now," my husband said, with a weary sigh.

He came into the room, and I pointed to the mess on the floor. He stared at it, for a moment, taking in the situation, and then, something happened, and humour took over: and there we were laughing together.

"Oh God, what a mess," I said.

"But you've got to admit it's funny," Chris said.

And God knows why – perhaps it was release of tension - but it was funny.

Writing this is very difficult; I try to remember words, and then a minute later those words evaporate. It reminds me of when I was writing my last book, *The Lupo Stick*, and it had become more and more stressful.

"You'll get there," my husband tells me. "You really will."

And, little by little, I am getting there. I do not allow him to alter a word that I have written. This is my story and my writing. This is me, this is how it is.
And I still quite like the me.

There are some beautiful moments in my life and I do not want it to end; at least, not at the moment.

TWENTY-THREE – WHERE DID I COME FROM?

The good thing is that my low bouts rarely last very long.

There is much to look forward to at the moment; the principal reason for this is the prospect of my daughter's wedding. After a difficult time she has finally found great happiness, and that means everything to me.

I should like to reminisce now,
on some childhood recollections.

Ingrid was about five and the dreaded question came up. I had been expecting it for a little while, and now, here it came:

"Mummy, where did I come from?"

I took a deep breath; "well," I told my daughter, carefully, mummy and daddy had a grown-up cuddle, and then like magic, it turned into you," I explained.

I could see her little face working away, trying to digest this monumental information, and frowning a little.

Then her forehead cleared: "Yes," she said excitedly. "And then daddy dug me out with a spade from your tummy," she said, in her funny little voice, that she had then.

It was all I could do to keep a straight face.

She has always had her own form of logic, a quirkiness that is unique to her. She had a very inquisitive mind; she loved to explore gadgets. The new toy, Lego, a doll that spoke – these toys all had to be examined in minute detail and five minutes later I would discover the item, dismantled.

"Oh dear," she would say, staring mournfully at the dismembered object. "It did it by itself."

And that was that.

I can recall another amusing incident: it would have been around the same time as the other one. We were walking down the road, and just then I spotted a dead bird. I prayed she wouldn't notice it. Of course, she did.

"What's that?" She asked me, stopping walking.

"It's a leaf, darling," I told her, trying to hurry her past.

She would not be hurried. In a matter of fact tone, she said, "No it's not. It's a dead bird," she corrected me. And she stared at it for a moment longer and we began walking again.

Growing up, life was not always easy for my lovely daughter. I was very young when I married my first husband; and the marriage did not last, which was my fault. I will always feel guilty for this; however, by the same token, there were also many happy times. The events to which I am alluding, were a very long time ago now, and my first husband, Irving, and myself are now the greatest of friends. I do realise that the early years cannot have been easy for her and that makes me very sad indeed. Despite everything however, she has thrived. She is a mother now, herself, and young Ruby is truly blessed to have such a good mother.

The one thing that matters more than anything to me is that Ruby will remember how her Grandma V used to be, before her Alzheimer's took over.

TWENTY-FOUR – THE QUARREL

Oh dear, what a quarrel Chris and I have just had. I hate quarrels and this one really wasn't my fault; it was about cooking. Now, I don't want to boast, but I have always been a good cook, however, as I have already mentioned I now need a lot of help in the kitchen. We usually rub along pretty well, considering the situation; the problem is that as Chris becomes more assured and I become less so, we tend to clash.

Years ago, my then boyfriend used to own a wine bar. I helped run it with him and did much of the cooking; hence I did not take kindly to being given advice by a mere novice. To use a cliché, it is akin to teaching your grandmother how to suck eggs. (And, by the way, I must remember to look up where that phrase originated from). On the menu for this evening, was penne pasta in a cheese sauce; however, today I was feeling particularly tired and muddled. My mind was feeling as though I was not really there. This happens to me when I am tired or stressed; but, by the same token I wanted to do the cooking myself; it was my own recipe, and I was protective of it. However, Chris's insisted I was not up to cooking this evening; I argued that I was fine and that I could make the cheese sauce with my eyes closed. Without a word he got out the ingredients and began to prepare making the food.

"Please, I want to do it myself," I persisted, close to tears.

"You're in a muddle," he said decisively."
And you're doing it wrong."

"I'm not, I'm really not." And I heard myself sounding like a thwarted child. "I can do it, I can. You have to let me." I was becoming overwrought now; and I attempted to take the bag of flour from him. My husband rarely raises his voice, but this time he did; we both ended up in tears.

There are lessons to be learnt from our squabble. I know that it must be very frustrating for Chris and I know he only has my best interests at heart, nonetheless it is important I do as much as I can.

And, by the way, the pasta was delicious.

TWENTY-FIVE — AIR-RAID SHELTER DAYS

Almost halfway down our long, narrow, garden is an old air raid shelter. Who had decided to site it there, and why, we will never know. I can only assume the shelter had been erected after a German aircraft had dumped its bombs over the bucolic fields of Moreton. There it stands in the midst of this tranquil hamlet, with all its proud memories. It has kept its secrets intact, forever a mystery, and now, only the dog plays there, standing high on his eyrie as he torments the pigeons.

I had the idea of making it into a den for the children in the village. It was a time of sweet innocence; young children, playing together, making up their own rules and dreams. There were usually five of them, though occasionally there were six. Their ages ranged from five, to nine, and they all lived within a minute of one another. When I first moved into Vine Cottage, all those years ago, the shelter was occupied by numerous spiders and mice. The cat had his own agenda. As far as he was concerned it was a free for all, and the mice did not stand a chance. I did feel sorry for them; they would be dispatched in the grizzliest of ways, poor things.

Over the next few weeks I scrubbed and swept, and painted. Soon it was unrecognisable. I had transformed it into a luxurious den, fit for the most pampered of children. The children celebrated with Mars bars and soft drinks. And of course, their favourite toys and Barbie dolls had to be there also.

I only wish my daughter had been of an age to have enjoyed those times.

I must tell you about my wonderful horse, Fleetwood, and how he is inextricably linked with the air raid shelter days. Earlier on I made reference to my beautiful horse, but the reason I have mentioned him again in this chapter, is because of the part that he played. The children in the village loved him and they were without any fear; and would take turns grooming him, whenever they had a chance. He was a large Anglo Arab and very gentle, and as the children rubbed his mane, his head would sink lower, and lower, in bliss. And sometimes I would hear the children early in the morning, before I had even got up. Fleetwood was a difficult horse to ride, as he had a tendency to bolt; yet he seemed to know when a child was on his back, because when I led him, he plodded along, peacefully, as though he were carrying a precious cargo.

The children came and went as they wished. It was an idyllic period, one which I will forever hold in my memory. Somehow the days seemed longer and brighter. And they merge together in my mind. Everyone knew everyone, and it would last for ever.

The children grew up, and no longer were they interested in Barbie dolls. Instead, there were images of pop stars pinned up on the walls of the shelter. Then, one by one, they ceased to come--better things to do with their time. And now they all have children of their own, and some have moved away. I hope they remember the air raid shelter days.

There is an aside to this: a few days ago I was walking the dog, and a stranger accosted me with a big smile; he was tall and there was a baby on his back.

"Hello, Valerie, he said,"
I looked at him without recognition and tilted my head.

"You don't recognise me do you?" He said.

"I'm so . . . I'm sorry," I began. Then all at once I realised who the handsome young man was, and the years rolled back and he was six years old. How could I have failed to recognise that great big grin of his? And the air raid shelter days came rushing back. And I listened to him say the magic words, "I will never forget those times."

MUSING ON MY ALZHEIMER'S

I should not complain,
after all, I am no longer young;
but why should I weakly submit
to the Machiavellian plans
you have in store for me.
I could rage, I could cajole,
but the brain we share is one and the same.
Privy to each other's thoughts and pain;
pugilists in all but name.
It has happened slowly, the rift between us,
a gradual drip, drip, the parting of our ways.
Bit by bit, an erosion
of that woman who was me.
Daily my parameters shrink, in a game of subtraction,
as the Brain Gremlins dance in glee.
And as I walk down the street,
conscious of my every timid step,
I am haunted by an abiding memory:
A young woman galloping on her horse,
laughing, free,
The capricious breeze tearing through her hair.
The rhythmic drumming of hooves beneath her feet.
Where did she go?
Long vanished on her Pegasus-steed.

TWENTY-SIX – FIRST EXCURSION

Chris has relented. After nine months of not allowing me to walk on my own, he has had to admit defeat. My nagging has finally paid off. The reason for my incarceration in the first place, was the corona virus. Chris was concerned that if I fell, no one would pick me up. I would be abandoned. People would step over me as if I didn't exist; I would be left by the wayside, like a leper. But now, oh joy, I am free.

Freedom, however, brings its own hazards; everything feels different, and within me there is a tight knot of fear. You are alone – except for your dog.

To begin with I felt ridiculously nervous; I tiptoed carefully, unused to my freedom.

"I have to do this," I told myself. "I have to."

Good, or bad, this is one of my traits: I will push myself and push myself to my limits, at all costs. It has now been nearly two weeks, and little by little, my confidence grows. I take time to appreciate my surroundings and I am aware that I have become more observant.

I can take in the sweet aroma of blossom; the scent of recent rain. I become acutely aware of the birdsong, and their different calls: the persistent sound of the robin, the great tit's distinctive teach-er, teach-er. With Elgar beside me, sniffing the tantalising smells and intermittently checking to make sure that I am still around, we walk on. And when I pass people in the lane they wave, and I may or may not know them, but it makes no difference. I feel alive.

TWENTY-SEVEN – FUR

Without doubt ours is surely the furriest household in the village. A long coat dog and a long coat cat compete with one another as to which of them is the hairiest, and who will leave the most fur on your clothes, or your person, on your favourite outfit. The innocent looking threads stick to you stubbornly, weaving patterns on your clothes. After tearing around the garden at break-neck speed, Elgar's lush fur becomes matted, and I spend the next hour painstaking de-matting him. And picking out tiny bits from the garden. I can spend more than an hour grooming, and he is amazingly patient considering the torture I am putting him through. This regime is repeated daily.

Bear, my Persian cat, slinks past me hoping to be invisible, and I grab him. He is in the same state as Elgar, but of course he has claws. I pinion his legs in readiness for a fight and, after this indignity, he disappears until he hears the rattling of his food bowl.

At this point, I think I should say a little about Bear. He is a very calm cat in general, and he rarely kills things, thank goodness; in another life he would have been a philosopher. He is a big, peach-coloured Persian, who most definitely rules the roost, and is governed by food.

Here is a list of some of his favourite delicacies: avocado pears, cucumber, red peppers (but not green peppers), potatoes, courgettes, which are his speciality. Oh, and not to forget cereal with raisins. It is important you realize that none of the above constitute his official diet, but are stolen.

It becomes something of a game; beady-eyed, bear will wait for his opportunity. This may come after Chris has prepared his muesli and has disappeared for a minute to get the newspaper. In that brief moment Bear will pounce. He will have jumped up onto the table and will have already have started on the muesli. At that point there will be a yelp of fury from Chris. But by then the cat will have fled.

TWENTY-EIGHT – STRANGE APPARITIONS

And now I am going to wind back time. I was about twenty-eight – but don't hold me to that, as my memory has a habit of playing tricks. It might have been more, or it might have been less.

The wine bar in Warwickshire was going from strength to strength; which is more than could be said for my relationship. Punishing hours and the endless quarrels took their toll, and we parted ways. But there is a reason why I am relating this. At the time we had the most beautiful old rectory in a remote village; it dated back to 1400, and had many original features. One of the rooms had a rather sinister atmosphere which made me quite shivery, particularly when I walked through the hall, in the evening.

My daughter was five or six at the time, and there were certain rooms which she did not like; in particular this applied to the attic. I had made this into a playroom and had put all her toys in there, thinking it would be perfect for her. However, she only ventured in there three or four times and then flatly refused to go near it again. Nothing would persuade her. And, in truth, I did not blame her; I, too, felt a strangeness in that attic.

I remember there was a grave virtually in our garden, and a narrow footpath with a right of way that almost abutted it. The footpath was rarely used; so when one day I went outside and saw a man staring upwards, almost in our garden, I asked him if he was lost. He came towards me, smiling.

"I used to live here," he explained.
"My father was the Vicar here."

I invited him indoors, and over coffee, we chatted.
When I asked him what he did, he told me that he
was a scientist. This surprised me.

"Was that awkward?" I asked him. "I mean, with you being
a scientist, and he a man of God?"

"Not at all," he told me. "The two are not incompatible,
and in fact, my mother used to hold séances where we
are now sitting."

Following on from what I have just written, I must tell you
about something extraordinary which happened a few
years ago. It was before James and I split up. I had taken
a photograph of him and my two dogs in the garden.
Several days later I collected the photos – in those days
this was a much more complicated process.

"Who is the woman in white? Is that you?" Said my friend,
when I showed her the pictures.

"No." I replied. "What are you talking about,
what woman?" I said.

My friend then pointed and I did a double take:
and peered hard. Clearly outlined in the picture was
a figure of a woman, in white, looking out from the window.
There were no obvious shadows, there had been just
James and the dogs; and now, there was this strange
woman in white. I don't know how one could explain

this phenomenon. Over the years I have shown this
photograph to many people, and the image is still
quite clear. I don't know how one can explain something
like this, without coming to the same conclusion; that this
was an apparition.

There is an appendage to this: fast forward twenty years.
A friend of mine came to visit. I had not seen him for
a long time.

"Did you know that your house was haunted?"
He asked me.

"I suspected it was," I said to him,
"but it was a long time ago, and I forgot about it."

"Well, let me tell you that it is."

And he went on to explain how friends of his had been
walking towards the footpath. A woman in white had
appeared from nowhere, and in utter silence, in front
of them, she had melted away.

Far fetched? I promise I am telling you the truth.
I still have the earlier photograph I had taken all
those years ago, and it all makes sense.

TWENTY-NINE – THE MISSING BABY

It is a Monday morning and the day has got off to a
rubbish start. First of all I could not find the dress which
I had wanted to wear, but then I remembered that I'd put it
in the washing machine, the day before, and I had not yet
taken it out. Then I spent half an hour searching for one of
my shoes; the dog was the obvious culprit, and I searched
high and low, but to no avail. Eventually, there was nothing
for it. I knew I would have to summon Chris – yet again.
He had that world-weary look on his face, poor man, and
my heart sank. I put on my sweetest, begging expression.

"I can't find where one of my shoes has got to.
It's gone AWOL," I told him.

"It's there, can't you see it? It's underneath the chair."

"Where?"

"Underneath the chair," he said again.
"Why can't you see it?"

"Alzheimer's," I sing out.

"You should be pleased I think you're normal,"
he said, smiling.

"Touché," I said, laughing.

Eventually, I set off with the dog, for our walk, which was
later than usual. I realized something just then, it must
seem that I'm always walking the dog. And here we are

again. We were very late setting off because of the mix-up with my clothes this morning. We took our usual route; the footpath was deserted, Elgar was off the lead, playing with a stick that was bigger than himself and making grunting noises in excitement. I do worry when he plays with sticks, in case they should get caught in his throat. But this was so big that I knew he would not come to harm. I watched for several minutes and I realised that I was laughing out loud at his antics. There was no one except my dog and me, and I wanted to shout out in exhilaration.

Elgar was some way away from me, and around the corner came a woman with a pram. Concerned that she might be anxious, I called out to her that my dog was no threat. Mindful of the pram, I walked towards her and caught up with her. Elgar had by now abandoned the stick and was once more by my side.

"What a lovely dog," the woman commented.

I thanked her then peered into the pram;
I could see no baby as yet, but assumed there was one.

"What a lovely baby," I commented. "Boy or girl?"

"He's a boy," the young woman said with a proud smile.

"He's very handsome," I told his mother,
and all the while my eyes were searching for a baby.

"How many months?"
I queried, beginning to feel rather frantic at this point.

"Five months today," she replied.
"Actually, where is he?"

"There," she said pointing.

"Where?"

"There!" With a frown.

I paused. And came clean. "I'm very sorry," I told her,
"but I can't actually see the baby." I hesitated a moment,
then explained. "I usually carry a white stick," I said to her,
"but I've had a bit of a stressful morning and I left it behind
today. I'm severely impaired due to an illness."

She was so kind then. She took my hand and placed it
on the baby's chest; there, as clear as daylight, was a
beautiful little baby who had been camouflaged by all
the toys within the pram. We chatted for a while after that,
and it transpired that she was a nurse and that she had
actually heard of PCA.

This incident was another important lesson for me;
I shall never try to pretend, and I really must stop bluffing.
I am what I am. I am who I am.

At what stage in life does one admit to old age? Is it a
sudden realisation? Is it because of a sudden pain or ache
that refuses to go? Perhaps it is when you become invisible
to other people, perhaps it is when you notice that you
have more grey in your hair than you realised. Is it when
you can no longer cut your own toenails?

Swallowing your pride you enlist your husband's help.
Is it when your daughter is about to turn fifty?
 – And how did that happen? And what about sex?

There you are. This is the same person that you always
were. The same girl, who cries, and who loves. I should
like to lie about my age, but who would care either way?
And you sift through the many years which had belonged
to you. You left me behind, you left me behind.

THIRTY – THE DEER

I would like now to share with you an amazing experience
which I had. I was still living in Warwickshire at the time
and it was only October. Except for my then dog, Zora,
I was alone in the house and dusk was fast approaching.
I was in the middle of making supper for myself when the
dog started barking frantically. I let him out, leaving the
back door open. I reasoned that no intruder would want
to take on my dog. Seconds later, he came tearing back,
his tail between his legs. Clearly he had had a bad shock,
and he was still trembling and cowering. I realized he must
have been disturbed by an animal; had it been a human he
would not have been afraid. I heard the sounds of banging
and crashing; it was like metal on metal.

And now I was frightened; I had no idea what I was
dealing with. I went in search of a torch, which took
several moments to locate. I could feel my own heartbeat
racing. Tentatively, I ventured outside. There, lit by the
torch, I saw a pair of antlers. Stunned, I realised the
creature was a deer. A huge Red Deer, which was rare
for the area where we lived. I presumed that the creature
was trapped, and I was at a loss as to what to do. I had
no idea how I would be able to release such a large animal.

And then, something incredible happened. In the semi
darkness, I could now make out, not one deer, but two.
The incredible, crashing, noise that I had heard, was
the coming together of the deers' antlers, locking and
unlocking, in combat.

All at once they heard me; for an instant they stopped dead. Then, in unison, they fled, in two different directions. For several minutes I stood there, marvelling at what I had been privileged to witness. I realised then, that, of course, it was the rutting season. And now there was no sign of the deer, and Zora ventured out once more, cautiously.

And now, staying with the animal theme, I must tell you of another remarkable incident. I was staying in the village of Stinsford, in Dorset, where I was researching for my novel, *Homage to Sarah*, and once again it was October. The museum was closed for the season, however, the museum curator kindly opened it for me. I spent an hour or so looking round, and then visited Thomas Hardy's gravestone in the local church. It was so peaceful, so beautiful. I had made myself a picnic in advance and went for a walk, searching for a suitable place to have my feast. Zora was with me, and we sat down on the moist grass, by a field gate, admiring the glorious view. Suddenly, I heard a drumming sound, as though I was being pursued. I turned to see what it was, and there in front of me was a beautiful fawn. Almost immediately, it began to frolic about around my dog, and minutes later they were playing together, leaping, springing and playing catch. Then, just as suddenly as it had appeared, the fawn scampered off.

I learnt later that the fawn had been orphaned and bottle fed by a family, under strict instructions that he must never be shot.

THIRTY-ONE – HOME

I wonder what it would be like to be another person and swap roles. For example, the very young would become the very old, and vice versa. Would we be better people for the experience? Perhaps we would be kinder, more tolerant, and more patient. This conundrum has, no doubt, fascinated philosophers for years, but for me, it is particularly interesting, as I pontificate on changes within myself.

I am continually wrestling with my brain to remember. Time has little meaning. Was it five years ago? Fifteen years ago? It means nothing, and I search the shadows of my brain, and time has no meaning any longer; and if I were to look at a calendar it provides me with no information, no date, no message. It is an empty book. The simplest words become a memory test. The days of the week sift uselessly through my fingers: and try to keep pace.

People say, "You look so well, you haven't changed,", "nobody would know", and "you sound so normal."

Oh, but you try filling the bath; you try making the bed; you try looking for cutlery; you try looking for the cupboard where the plates are kept.

Like many people, I have always dreamt of living in Cornwall. However, naturally, one's circumstances will play a big part in where one ends up living. Usually, one lives somewhere by default. In my case, I could not have left my elderly mother who lived near Marlow, in Buckinghamshire.

When she died, I realised that due to my own illness, I needed to be surrounded by familiarity. To begin with this was a blow; Chris and I had both lived with the Cornish dream for so long. We tried to convince ourselves that it could work. We looked in the magazines and online, drooling over converted fishermen's cottages, imagining ourselves rushing into the sea. We had established that there were good train services to Truro, and there were good doctors' surgeries nearby, and a thriving little community. But then there was a spate of bad weather. We imagined ourselves differently now: we knew nobody. Friends that we had nurtured over years were miles away. My daughter was miles away. The sea was dark and frightening; nothing was familiar; if one of us was ill, who would we turn to in an emergency? Suddenly, the idyll looked sharply different, and in that sobering moment we realized we had had our chance. We pictured winter and isolation, and strangers who would not be interested in us. Then we pictured our beautiful thatched cottage and our peaceful hamlet that terminated at the farm.

And here I am now. Everyone knows my situation; and when they see me they let me know who they are, because otherwise, I would not recognise them. And this is our idyll. This is where circumstances have brought us.

And the funny thing is, as we walk along the footpath, there is a section that reminds us of Cornwall.

THIRTY-TWO – THE WINE TRADE

My father had been in the wine trade all his life, as had his father before him. It was a long, established, business. My great grandfather had come to England from Latvia as a refugee. Being an astute businessman, he secured the rights for a popular liqueur called *Kummel*. After his death, my grandfather, in turn, developed the business, importing fine French wines. My father then expanded the business further, by incorporating more general wines, and also wines under the company's own label, called *Arc de Triumph*. This was shipped over and kept under bond, and I can still hear the clink, clink of the bottles, as they made their way along the bottling line.

I joined the business in 1975, as part of the sales team. Over the years, I learnt a lot about wines and the wine industry; I was fortunate to have such an interesting job, and I enjoyed being on the sales side of the business. I met many interesting people and travelled extensively around the Home Counties, which I really enjoyed. My dog was always in the car with me, and he was definite asset. We had a large premises in Neasden which took up about four acres. I knew everyone who worked there, and the atmosphere was one of geniality and light-hearted banter.

My own biggest success was when I managed to secure the contract to one of the country's largest supermarket chains. I remember those years as particularly happy times. I would knock at my father's door, and his face would light up when he saw it was me. I would tell him my strategy for the day, and he would comment accordingly. The staff all respected him, and he was always fair.

And now, I have a couple of anecdotes that I think warrant relating.

It was winter – soon to be Christmas. I was doing the rounds of some of my clients; and the last on the list was a theatre. The theatre itself was a converted mill and it involved climbing up four levels of steps to reach the admin department. With four bottles of wine in my arms, I began to climb. Breathless, I finally reached the top. I bent down to locate the door handle – and that was when it happened:

I was wearing a voluminous Poncho, and to my dismay it became trapped in the door frame. I was stuck. I could either drop the bottles of wine and release the door, or be forced to rip my new poncho to pieces in an effort to release myself. What a dilemma. I looked around but could see and hear no one. Help, help! I cried out feebly, when, hallelujah, I heard footsteps coming up the stairs. It was the woman who I dealt with. She took one look at me and, upon seeing my predicament, burst out laughing, then released me.

There is a second and final anecdote,
which I thought might amuse.

I had been asked to take over the wine contract for the Police Staff College at Bramshill, at short notice, and had booked an appointment accordingly. After being checked in by security, I then made my way up a couple of flights of stairs, clutching two samples of wine, one red and one white. I was halfway down the corridor when I became aware that my tights were slithering downwards. I peered about me. The coast was clear. Carefully, I laid down the bottles of wine, and, one by one, I hauled up the legs of my wayward tights. Much more comfortable now, I picked up the two bottles, and full of confidence, swanned into the room.

As I entered, gales of male laughter and clapping greeted me. I was baffled, completely taken back for a minute or two. Then it dawned on me. How could I not have realised that there would be security cameras everywhere in a place like this? I remember exclaiming, out loud, "Oh No!" And then I joined in the laughter. It was an unusual form of getting a new contract.

THIRTY-THREE – A REAL WRITER

My father retired in 1985. He had sold the business by then, and nothing was the same. Without my father at the helm, everything was very different. Not only was the company name changed, but the very ethos and way of working was different. The changing of the name was the final straw, and I, too, resigned.

Parallel to my job, for the last several years, I had been writing a novel. I wrote every spare minute that I could; it was a compulsion. I could not believe that one day I might actually be published. I'd already had a couple of rejections, albeit encouraging ones. I had to face facts; I needed to be pragmatic. Thus, I set about finding a new career for myself.

In my younger days I had been a model. There was now quite a demand for older models, and I did consider going down that road. In the end, I decided it wasn't for me and I enrolled for an interior design course. It was in Bath, which would not have been the most practical of places to commute to each day, but the course was only for two weeks and, besides, I enjoyed driving in those days, and the drive to Bath was beautiful.

I had looked into the course itself and it seemed exactly the sort of thing that I was looking for. Importantly, I would be my own boss, which is what I was used to when I was working for my father.

The course did not start for two months, and this gave me time to establish contacts, meeting with designers and opening accounts with them. I am absolutely hopeless at maths, and knew that I would never be able to work out the terrifying intricacies of pattern cutting. The good news was that I had recently met a pattern cutter, which would solve the problem.

In case you are becoming bewildered by talk of pattern cutting and fabrics, worry not: it is leading to something really extraordinary. I had hired two young men to decorate my cottage, using special effects. It needed decorating anyway, so it was an ideal chance to test their skills. Their work was excellent – they were real artisans, and I told them that I would like to use them for my future business.

"There's just one thing I should mention," I told them. "I have just finished writing a novel. I doubt it will come to anything, but if it were to be taken up, I wouldn't be using you, as obviously I would be focusing on my writing."

The older of the young men said, "That's interesting. My aunt is a publisher."

My ears pricked up. "Who is she with?" I asked, and he told me her name.

It was the publisher who was interested in my book.

Just five minutes later, the telephone rang. It was my literary agent.

And so the first people to hear the news that my book had been accepted were currently painting my room.

"I'm so sorry, but I shan't be using you," I told them, laughing with joy and disbelief. The coincidence was, I'm sure you would agree, truly extraordinary.

I shall never forget the euphoria I experienced that day. That first novel, *To Anna, About Whom Nothing Is Known*, took six years to write because of my full-time job. Ironically, this was about the same length of time it had taken me to write my last novel, *The Lupo Stick*.

I remember celebrating, with all my wonderful family around me, that evening.

Oh, how long ago that was.

THIRTY-FOUR – TODAY

I have to admit that it is becoming harder and harder to write this. Using Siri is nearly impossible now, as I keep going on to the wrong command button. Sometimes I feel like giving up, but then just when I feel I can't take any more of it, something propels me forward and drives me on. So, here I go again. It's a funny world. Who decides which way to go?

I have just had the most awful experience. It is so hard to explain and I'm not sure I shall be able to. I woke up this morning as usual, at about 7:30, and I headed for the toilet. I was very wobbly and confused and, whilst on the one hand I knew where I was and I could talk, on the other hand I found myself totally unable to function. I was completely *compos mentis*. I could feel my brain working, yet I could not turn on the wretched tap. I could see the toilet in front of me; I could see the actual bath, but, even though both were staring at me, I simply did not know what to do. All I could do was stand there hopelessly. As I write this I can feel again, the horrible panic that arose within me. There was I, standing in the middle of the bathroom unable to do anything. It was as though I was paralysed; as though my whole body had gone into a kind of seizure. I knew I should be able to turn the taps on, but they just seemed to look at me, mocking. I was aware of myself pacing around, as though for inspiration, picking up things, putting them down again, staring, just staring. I don't know how long this lasted – it was probably about quarter of an hour or more – but then, gradually, I could feel my body returning to the person who is me.

I'd had a few similar bouts to this before, but they had never been this bad. I decided I should contact my doctor. I was suspicious that I might have had a TIA, which is like a mini stroke; however, over the phone, the doctor went through various tests with me. She told me that I had not had a stroke; none of the symptoms applied to me.

Whilst I was reassured to know that I had not suffered a TIA, I knew, without being told, that my Alzheimer's had taken several turns for the worse. I have an appointment booked in a month's time with the neurologist, but I know myself. I know my body back to front, and surely, that is my cue for a joke.

THIRTY-FIVE – FRENCH JOURNEY

I have been searching and searching, for a diary that
I had written about 30 years ago. It has apparently gone
into space. My search has taken me into places I had long
forgotten and it was tempting for me to be distracted,
but no, I have to remain focused, and I continued to
search. After several days I have to concede defeat.
The diary is lost for good.

The diary in question charted an unusual holiday I had
taken in France. There were two reasons for my French
adventure: the first was to research my then novel,
Kempton's Journey, which I was writing, the second,
was simply a whim.

I had seen an advertisement in a national paper,
which had caught my eye.

*Explore the beautiful Lotte et Garonne area of France in
a gypsy caravan, at your own leisurely pace, and recapture
another era as your horse plods along in front of you.*

Well, how could I resist that? In my mind I was already
picturing it--just me and a horse, drinking in all the luscious
scenery, and meeting people I would never normally meet.
I wasted no time. There and then I contacted the woman
who had placed the advertisement.

But, as usual I have jumped the gun. The holiday would
begin with the wine area of Bordeaux, and here is the

problem: my diary, with all-my long ago notes, is missing. I therefore have to trust to a very shaky memory.

But, no. Not quite! Just now I have unearthed some of the notes I had made, all those years ago for my book *Kempton's Journey*. So here goes.

The taxi from Bordeaux airport deposits me near the station. The quay is a hive of sound and activity, a cacophony of jangling chains, tapping masts, rattling rigging, and water slapping gently against hulls. Brown-armed men load and unload wooden crates from cargo boats, hammering, banging, whistling. A fisherman mending his net – and feet skirting past me. Warm southern faces. The reek of fish and spilled wine, of soot and traffic. And beyond the tangle of boats and the irregular line of warehouses and factory chimneys, is the sweep of the Garonne. I take it all in, enchanted.

It's almost time for my train. I drag my case along the platform as a TGV draws up, then dashes off. A couple of minutes later my train draws up, more leisurely, and I climb inside and find a seat. My eyes are riveted to the window, and the pretty countryside which unfolds like a carpet. It takes in various small rural stations on its journey to Bergerac.

And now the countryside evens out, becoming flatter; and the interminable vineyards with their gnarled stumpy vines have given way to farmland, with smallholdings amongst the patches of green. It has been a long day, and without realising it, I fall asleep. I am woken by the ticket collector demanding to see my ticket, which was just

as well, as otherwise I might have ended up who knows
where? I get off ten minutes later at Saint-Émilion,
where I would be staying for three days.

Saint-Émilion was a charming village and a world Heritage
site, nestling in the heart of the wine growing area of
Bordeaux. I had booked myself into a small pension there,
but it had been a long day and I was too weary to explore;
there would be time for that during my stay.

I shall always associate macaroons with Saint-Émilion. Their
sweet aroma seemed to embrace the entire village. After
all these years, I can still conjure up the sweet, pungent
smell in my nostrils. The smell of the baking macaroons
early in the morning permeated the entire village.

I went downstairs for breakfast. There was only one other
couple in the small dining room: a well-endowed woman
whose partner's eyes kept straying to her breasts.
The woman was feeding morsels to her little poodle,
and was oblivious to her partner. After a few minutes,
an inner door swung open and the owner of the auberge
appeared, wearing a white apron around his waist.
He gave a beaming smile at seeing me.

"Bonjour Mademoiselle, did you sleep well?
What would you like for breakfast?"

And now I was presented with a dilemma: croissants,
or macaroons? Needless to say, I had both.

I spent a leisurely morning wandering about. Saint-Émilion
was a town of almost staggering beauty. It resembled a toy

village. Stone gates allow you entry into the old part of the town. Saint-Émilion was named after a monk, who had fled persecution and lived in a cave for 17 years. Over the years, other monks joined him, and the reputation of the wine they had created, spread. I was shown around the underground catacombs by a guide; these led to the underground church.

After an hour or so, I surfaced from the darkness of the sinister catacombs, adjusting my eyes to the bright sunlight and the bustle of cafés and shops. The Bell Tower soared above me, and at that moment the bell rang out.

On my second day, I had planned a visit to a vineyard, followed by a wine tasting. There were half a dozen or so of us, and everyone was very serious and reverent. One man even took notes. I daresay you know the type. I felt as though I was back at school. I myself had given wine tastings and lectures, but I had always included something amusing to lighten up the mood. Guests sipped and slurped, passing comments and nodding their heads in knowledgeable agreement. I saw myself emulating the others, as we spat our way through the various wines; and I bit my lip hard to prevent myself from laughing out loud. I think it was the seriousness of the occasion that had prompted me to react as I did: I suddenly realised how funny we all must have looked, spitting away, not always accurately.

On the final day, I had the good fortune to meet a couple of university students. We struck up a instant rapport, and they insisted on showing me around the area, and so, in their ancient Citroen 2CV, we bumped and rattled along the narrow, uneven roads. The vineyards stretched for mile upon mile; in between gaps you would catch a glimpse of magnificent manor houses and the familiar names of the vineyards would be embellished on them.

We had been driving for more than an hour; the river was now parallel to us, and running high. My hosts stopped at a large sign which informed us that we were now in Entre-Deux-Mers. Literarily, Entre-Deux-Mers means, between two rivers. The area was famed for its beauty. The three of us got out of the car. The sound of water was everywhere.

We found our way back via a different route, and bumped our way back in the Citroen, to Saint-Émilion. I treated my new friends to coffee and macaroons. Then we parted company, vowing to stay in touch. Of course, we meant it at the time – one always does, but sadly, I did not see them again.

Writing this has brought back many memories, and I wonder, anew, what happened to those lovely students who had had nothing to gain by entertaining me that day.

And now for the next part of my journey. I left Saint-Émilion for the town of Bergerac, the following day, with some regret but also excitement. The weather was unusually cool for the time of year, which did not augur well. And now I worried that I had not packed sufficient warm clothes. Too bad. There was nothing now that I could do about it. I had packed my oil paints, I had packed my bikini, but I had only packed one jumper. The train swayed with a clacketing rhythm, and myself with it, as it passed through various small rural stations on its route to my destination. Outside, the weather had turned an ominous dark grey.

On arriving at Bergerac I was met by the proprietor, Danielle, who'd placed the advert I had first seen. She was instantly recognisable by her battered Renault which she had described on the phone to me. Danielle was half French and half English and she would veer seamlessly from one language to the other. She was a small woman in her early 50s, who did not stop talking, and she barely stopped for breath. She lived, so she informed me almost immediately, with her female lover and business partner.

Her farmhouse was half an hour's drive from Bergerac, near the small Bastide town of Monflaquin. As we clambered out the car, several dogs rushed through the yard towards us, scattering chickens. A woman followed at a less hurried pace. She was also short stout, with cropped grey hair, face creased in a smile. When she spoke it was in an upper-class English accent.
She introduced herself as Tanya.

A fire snapped and crackled in the cavernous fireplace. The cottage was full of character.

"We did it up all ourselves," Tanya explained proudly, when I comment on it.

We discussed arrangements. Every day I would be stopping off with the horse at a different farm or auburge; at the end of each day, one of the women would fetch me by car and take me to a different location for the night. Meanwhile, the horse would happily be resting in a field until the next morning. Danielle explained that I would only ever be a maximum of twenty miles from the farm. In effect, I would be making a circle around the Bastide towns. I remember how impatient I was to get going.

Danielle led out the horse from the field. Bella was a white Percheron mare, with a backside the size of a buttress. My own horse would have been dwarfed in comparison. Bella stood quietly without being held while was harnessed. I remember feeling a sense of misgiving at the sight of all the paraphernalia required for the harness, and thinking that I would never get the hang of it. I had not considered the technicalities, and I watched Danielle position the saddle pad on Bella's back.

Under Danielle's instruction I managed to put the neck collar on. Next came the bridle, which I was used to, and the metal bit slipped neatly into her mouth.

The most difficult part for me was fitting the harness to the caravan. This was easier said than done and required several attempts, circling her until she was exactly central, then coaxing her backwards. The caravan itself was painted red, with a swirling blue and yellow design. There was a rounded metal roof whose overlapping sides formed a protective shield against the weather.

Danielle and I piled in our bits of luggage, along with grooming kit and a large rock, to prevent the wagon from rolling when parked on a hill.

And now we were off. Under Danielle's supervision, I took the reins from her. I had assumed that the driving itself would be easy, but Bella sensed instantly I was a novice, and took advantage of my lack of experience. She meandered along lethargically, at one stage, stopping to graze from the verge.

"You need to be much firmer with her," Danielle told me.

Gradually I began to relax a little, and to feel some contact with her head. Bella's enormous white rump rolled from side to side, rhythmically. The steady clumping of her feet; the creaking of the caravan; the undulating countryside – I was acutely aware of all of these. At the back of my mind lurked the thought that if we stopped for more than a second, the caravan would roll backwards. I shifted my position to make it more central, and made sure I could reach the handbrake easily if necessary. And now I could feel my confidence growing and began to enjoy myself.

It took me four days before I was sufficiently competent at driving, but Danielle remained with me throughout, in case of any trouble. On the one hand I would have liked to have been by myself, but I had to accept that this would not have been responsible, particularly as roads were very narrow and although traffic was almost non-existent, when a car did materialize at some speed, I had to simultaneously apply the handbrake whilst dealing with the horse.

Looking back at that time in France, I marvel at myself then. I had no fear, just a sense of excitement and adventure. I met so many people on the way; I met so many characters, and my recollections come fast and furiously at me now.

My first stop off point for that evening was a farm, in an isolated spot. I was greeted by the farmer, a stocky little man, with a complete lack of teeth, except for a gold one in the middle. He smiled a great deal, emphasising his single tooth, and he immediately launched into French with a strong local dialect. To begin with, I understood not one word; he didn't seem put out, and continued to rabbit on. In return, I did lots of gesticulating, grinning, and nodding. He seemed quite satisfied with that and between us, we managed to communicate.

I gathered that his wife would be arriving shortly, and we muddled on as best we could. Then, a strange thing happened: I became aware that I could understand everything he was saying; I found my knowledge of French returning as though by magic, and I ceased to feel self-conscious.

After twenty minutes or so, his wife arrived, and she showed me into the room that I would be occupying for the night. It was spotlessly clean, and above the bed was a large picture of Christ, looking very sanguine, considering all that he had been through. Unlike her husband, the wife spoke some English, and I gathered that she had a job in the nearby village. She told me that dinner would be ready within half an hour. She called me for supper, and I went downstairs.

The table was elegantly laid for the three of us; then I noticed it: a very long, wiggly, eel. In advance I had explained that except for fish, I was vegetarian. Not in a month of Sundays, however, could I have imagined that eel would be on the menu. I could feel myself blanching.

139

"You like eel?" She asked me, with a happy smile,
and clearly she thought that she was presenting me
with a great delicacy.

I could only stare at the eel with horror, and hope that
she would mistake it for enthusiasm. I picked at it as best I
could, forcing a grin of appreciation, and trying not to gag.

The next day was rainy and cold. I managed to connect
the horse to the wagon, which was very satisfying.
However, my fingers were numb and slippery, and
Danielle and I, huddled under the overhang of the roof,
together. Bella plodded on, but her ears were set back,
and I could tell that she was unhappy.

"What's happened to the weather?" I asked Danielle,
shivering involuntarily.

"It's La Lune Russe," she explained ruefully, pulling a face.

"La Lune, what?" I questioned.

"La Lune Russe," Danielle said again.
"It's a phenomenon which occurs every few years.
Literally, it means the Russian Moon."

I thought longingly of all my nice warm clothes at home.
How stupid I had been fantasising that I would be wearing
a bikini, and painting in the open. Danielle must have read
my mind.

"I'll lend you a warm jumper," she volunteered.

We soldiered on, despite the weather. There were windows of sunshine, and we took advantage of these to eat our picnic. A grey mist shrouded the countryside, and it was difficult not to feel despondent. My dread was that the entire week would be like this. We made small talk for a while, but, really, there was nothing much to say.

"I think it will be a bit better tomorrow," Danielle told me, trying to sound optimistic. "At least that's what the weather forecast showed."

"I wouldn't put money on it," I said grimly.

We led Bella to the field for the night; it was much bigger than the one before, and in addition, she had company: a very small Shetland pony, no bigger than a large dog. The pair went crazy together, whinnying with joy when they saw one another, then kicking up their heels and cavorting in happiness. Clearly they knew each other well, and were friends; it was a delight to see them frolicking and, at that point, the sun came out and they lowered themselves onto their haunches, and both of them rolled, one way, then the other, then shaking themselves, began to graze, and with it, my mood lightened. How could anyone be so ignorant as to say that animals do not have feelings?

The venue for that evening was an old inn. The owner greeted me with a cigarette dangling with from her lips. A long line of men's slippers was the first thing that caught my attention. The shoes resided in one part of a large room, the slippers on the opposite side. They were, as I later discovered from Danielle, known as 'Lottie Gironde' slippers and the men donned them as soon as they entered the inn. An old greyhound snored in a corner of the room.

As I walked through, heads turned in my direction; I felt like an intruder, as, other than the owner, I was the only woman there. They made no attempt to hide their curiosity, or was it disapproval? I could not tell. All I know is that I have never felt more uncomfortable. The entire room had become silent. However, after half an hour, most of the men had dispersed and I read quietly in a corner of the room.

The owner's son, a silent, wary individual, brought me my evening meal, with a curt "Bon appetite." I remember it was a delicious Bouillabaisse. I thanked him, and received a nod in return. To take my mind off the strange atmosphere, I gazed at all the pictures of horses and dogs that were framed and displayed on the wall.

I did not sleep well at night, for two reasons: the first was because the room stank of nicotine, the second was the owner's hacking cough. In addition, the lavatory was down a long corridor, and the light was on a timer; it had a nasty habit of timing out just as I was about to use it. I confess that when I needed it again, I used the basin.

The next morning I awoke to hear whistling. Somebody was whistling a perfect rendition of the *Queen of the Night*. It is fiendishly difficult to sing, let alone whistle to, with such accuracy.

I went down to breakfast.

"Was that you whistling the *Queen of the Night*?"
I asked the young man.

He looked askance at me,
then admitted that it had been him.

"You like music?" He asked me.

I nodded in affirmation
and his demeanour changed completely.

"Right, I shall test you now," he said.

"Go on then," I dared him.

This time he whistled to the tune of *Samson* from *Samson and Delilah.*

"Well that's easy," I told him.
"That is from *Samson and Delilah.*"

And now he laughed. He treated me to a tour of the house, and it transpired that all the pictures that I had admired earlier were of racehorses that he had owned over the years, and likewise the dogs. He was a well-known jockey and the pictures were of his winners. And now, we were the best of friends. We talked about music, and about horses and dogs, and breakfast was on the house.

There are so many stories and tales I could recount regarding my French odyssey; far too many to recount here, and I would not want to bore you. But I met so many interesting people – kind people, eccentric people, fascinating people. I think this is where I should finish at this point. Suffice to say that I still cherish my memories of my French adventure. Oh, and in case you are wondering, La Lune Russe lasted the entire time, but Bella was kept snug in her New Zealand rug. What is a bit of rain, compared to the experience I had?

THIRTY-SIX – NO MORE GETTING LOST

It has happened again. That is three times, within a short space of time; three times that I have got lost. I know that it is because I am not concentrating. I am easily diverted and my mind drifts. Sometimes I think that I have a sieve for a brain. I used to be familiar with every detail of this beautiful area where I have the good fortune to live. The gentle, undulating, narrow tracks and paths; the brook meandering through the meadows; open farmland, and grazing, curious cows, munching on the lush grass.

And now I realize I am lost again. It is the swallow's fault. It came as such a surprise as it flitted past me, this tiny bird which has flown thousands of miles. What motivates him? I'm back, he cries, I remember you.

I can go left, or straight ahead. I opt for the latter. I continue walking. I hear squeals of joy, excited children, and the barking of dogs. I seem to have been walking endlessly, in a big circle, for ages, but those sounds mean I must be close to the recreation ground. I sigh with relief, and turn back on myself.

Two hours later, back home, I face Chris's wrath.

"Where have you been? I've been going frantic," he demands.

"I met a lot of people," I told him, not meeting his eyes.

"You got lost again," he accused me.

"Sort of," I admit. "But I'm fine."
And I explain about the swallow.

"Right, that's it," my husband told me.
"I'm going to get a tracking app for your phone."

"You are bloody well not," I retorted.

"Yes, I am," he insists, becoming frustrated with me.
It ends with a quarrel, and tears on my part.

But gradually I have accepted it; it was either that,
or never letting me walk on my own. Gradually, I am
realising that it is the right thing to do. Just another
dent in my independence.

"I can't even have an affair now," I teased him.

But, in truth, I am glad of the device. Without being
aware, I had been losing my confidence. The fact he
knows where I am is comforting and gives me a warm
feeling, especially as my speech now sometimes lets me
down, and I become almost inarticulate. If I need to ask
someone the way, it is likely that I will fight for the words,
and become even more confused in my agitation.

Tomorrow is our wedding anniversary: thirteen years.
That is not to be sniffed at. In actuality we have known
one another twice that length of time. We celebrated
yesterday, a Saturday; razzle dazzle night. Who wants
to celebrate on Monday when nobody is about? In
addition, this will be the first time we will have been out
to a restaurant for more than a year, due to Covid, and

lockdown. It feels weird, somehow. It feels as though I am a child breaking a strict rule. I feel as though there is a kind of nakedness all around me. My Alzheimer's accentuates this strange sensation.

THIRTY-SEVEN – WEDDING BELLS

As the day of my daughter's wedding draws closer,
so my nervousness creeps up on me again. I dislike
myself for this. I should be so excited – and I am, I really
am. It is just that a nameless terror seems to be taking
over me. It should not be like this; my beautiful girl is all
that matters. Her happiness is all that matters. And her
chosen partner in life is, I know, the right man for her.
However, over the years I have developed a fear of crowds
and noise, which is due to my Alzheimer's becoming worse.

And now the day itself has arrived, and Chris helps
me get dressed for the occasion. All I can think is,
what if I need to go to the loo? Who will take me?

We have hired a taxi, rather than driving ourselves –
less stressful. The driver arrives on time and I gingerly
climb into the car. We had estimated that it would take
an hour and a half at least to drive to London,
from Oxford, allowing for traffic.

I picture my daughter: at this moment she will be at the
hairdressers. What are her thoughts? Is she nervous?
I long to be with her. I wish it could have been me,
helping her on with her dress, that we had chosen
together. I wish I could be there to calm her nerves.
Never have I felt more useless and inadequate.
We could have been together, I could have felt part
of the occasion, rather than a guest, but I would have
been of little use. And I know that if she were reading
this she would understand.

And now we are on the M40. London looms;
countryside vanishes. Familiar names flash past
and my stomach tightens.

Without realising it I had fallen asleep for a few minutes.
I awake with a sense of disorientation; my brain is unable
to absorb what is happening. Traffic; hooting of cars; the
squealing of articulated lorries and buses. All these register
in my mind. And now we are passing Uxbridge, the start
of London. Every sound, every detail registers in my brain,
before it disappears. All of a sudden I have a recollection
that makes me gasp, it is so vivid: as a treat, my grandpa
had taken me to the open air swimming pool in Uxbridge.
I remember the shrieks of joy and the splashing of water;
I would have been about eight at the time and had just
learnt to swim. Afterwards, I was allowed a cornet.
The memory fades.

Now we are passing the North Circular turn off.
The smells of London; boarded up shops; queues for fast
food; advertising hoardings and graffiti; and tatty houses
and flats, with washing hanging out to dry in the breeze.
The car speeds onwards, and my stomach with it. I used
to love going into London: memories of the theatre, opera,
and musical shows, with my parents. Getting off the train
at Marylebone would herald the start of a day in London.
But all that has changed. I have become a country bumpkin
and I feel out of place and threatened. I want to run back
home, like a frightened hare. The crowds and noise bear
down on me.

We arrive at the synagogue at 3:45 PM – we are a half an
hour early, we are always early! But it does not matter;

it gives us a chance to admire the beautiful old synagogue, and for me to get my bearings. I can feel myself beginning to relax a little. And now, guests are beginning to arrive. Amongst them I recognise several of Ingrid's old school friends. They had been children then and now they have children of their own. When they were young, some of them used to stay with us, and it is lovely to see them again, as adults. It takes me right back and I can feel my eyes watering.

By now the groom has arrived, looking remarkably calm. Other guests are fast arriving. Any minute now, my daughter will be coming through with her father, on her arm.

And there she is; walking at a slow pace towards the Huppah, with two bridesmaids behind her. Weeping at your daughter's wedding may be a cliché. You do your utmost not to, but there you are, suddenly blubbing and grinning simultaneously. She looks regal and very beautiful. Being a traditional Jewish wedding, she takes her place at the Huppah and smiles at her husband to be. The Rabbi opens the proceedings with a moving homily, and this is followed by the Cantor's beautiful singing. After this, the bride has to circle her husband-to-be, seven times. This is symbolic: this is to assure the groom that he is marrying the right woman and is not being duped!

The service finishes with more wonderful singing from the Cantor, then finally the famous breaking of the glass, by both parties. Muzzletoff, Muzzletoff, came the clapping and laughter from around the room.

We emerge from the synagogue, blinking in the bright sunlight, and wait for the coach, which will ferry us to the R.A.F. Club. This will be our venue for the reception. Walking through into the historic building, one has a sense of grandeur. Paintings of aircraft adorn the walls, in commemoration of the RAF.

The evening progresses, champagne flows, and now it is time for the speeches. Ingrid's father gives an emotional address, followed by Alan, in fine fettle, as one would expect. I would like to have made a speech also;
but I would not have been able to read it,
let alone remember the words.

Throughout the meal, I need help from Chris.
I keep dropping pieces of food to the floor and I am deeply embarrassed and ashamed, but cannot help it.
I think everyone must be staring at me.
I have said it before: Alzheimer's knows no shame.

The arrival of the Wedding Cake causes a stir and laughter, as together, the Bride and Groom cut the cake with a ceremonial sword.

But now the car has arrived. It is time to leave; what a day it has been. Emotional for me, of course; happiness on behalf of my daughter. And as we leave the lights of London, I hold my husband's hand so tightly, oh so tightly.

THIRTY-EIGHT – MY FATHER

Today would have been my father's birthday. He would
have been a hundred and two. Without a doubt, we
would have been celebrating. My father was a great
believer in celebrating. Whatever the occasion, he
needed no excuse to bring out the champagne.
He was a family man, and family was everything to him.
He was also a very emotional man, and as my mother's
dementia deteriorated, he found it increasingly hard to
hide his distress and, increasingly, he reached out to me
for moral support, and this brought us very close.

Then, I recall him ringing me up one day, in despair.

"I can't make her understand where the bedroom is,"
he said, almost in tears. "She will not budge,
and she is accusing me of bullying her."

He put me on the phone to my mother, and I managed
to persuade her by changing the subject completely.
It was very sad to witness her deterioration. I expect
people say the same thing about myself; but as I have
explained, with PCA Alzheimer's, cognitive function
remains largely intact. A philosophical question: what is
worse, to be unaware of your faculties and therefore
refuse to believe that you have any impairment?
Or is it preferable to comprehend everything around
you, yet you cannot perform the most basic of tasks?

To return to my father: I recall a particular day. I was about
to drive to Winchester. Every summer, once a year, I was
invited to lecture at the annual writer's conference. It was

a prestigious event, and I focused my lecture on how to bring characters to life. It always draws a large audience.

"Drive carefully," my father instructed me, hugging me tight.

"I shall do," I promised, and I set off.

As the journey progressed I felt ill at ease, and I realised I was driving in the centre of the road. For no reason at all, I could feel myself becoming nervous. I felt myself breaking into a sweat. People were hooting at me in anger, and I swerved, narrowly missing a van.

My father's words rang in my head. Drive carefully. Drive carefully. And only now, as I write this, do I realise that this might have been the beginning of my PCA. This means that I must have had the disease longer than I thought. I arrived back home safely, but shaken, after my long day.

It was a two-day seminar, and my dog came with me; he was a great attraction and very popular in between lecture breaks. I took him for walks on the nearby downs. Then we would resume, and he would sit at my feet. It was all very relaxed and informal, and I daresay that people thought I was a bit eccentric. It was a truly lovely time and I made some good friends. It has changed now, it is part of the University, and for sure, I wouldn't have been able to teach with a dog in tow!

The organiser, Barbara Large, became a friend, but as life changed for me, we lost touch. I was very sad to learn recently that she had died.

But you see how I jump about from one thing to another! I started this piece about my father and so, I would like to close it in a similar vein.

Happy birthday to my beloved Father, happy birthday.

THIRTY-NINE – TRAVELS WITH MY DOG

Oh dear, never ask for directions from somebody who is severely sight impaired! I am halfway through a walk with Elgar - and by the way, this stupid machine has just interpreted the word Elgar as alcohol – when I am accosted by a man and a woman who are lost.

It is very hot day and they look harassed and hot.
I have the impression that they have been arguing.
The woman approaches me – you will never see a man asking the way. "Sorry to bother you," she asks politely, "but do you know the way to Chinnor?"
She seems oblivious to my white stick.

"Oh my goodness, you're miles away," I commented.

"Well that's a fat lot of good," the man mutters.
And the woman glares at him.

I try to picture the route, meanwhile.

"You need to turn round then, and carry on up the footpath. When you come to the crossroads, turn right, and keep going for about a mile.
Then you will see a sign post for Chinnor."

My instructions do seem logical to me. And I want to sound business-like. I reason that they can always ask someone else further on. Elgar and I continue our walk with a clear conscience. Back home I explain to Chris the route I had suggested to them.

Chris looked askance.

"But that's nowhere near the way to Chinnor," he said. "You've sent them in the opposite direction."

"Have I really?" I said. And then, to my shame, I fall about laughing. Anyway, in mitigation, surely they should have noticed my white stick.

I go into the garden to do some weeding. Gardening has become something of a challenge nowadays. I pluck out a particularly vicious-looking weed. At that moment, Chris happens to look up, and gives a strangulated yelp. How was I to know that the weed which I had just pulled out, was in fact a carefully planted geranium.

We are fortunate to have a large garden, with plenty of shade. For Chris's birthday a few years ago, I commissioned a friend to make a wooden table; on it were the words, 'Christopher's birds'. Chris is very dutiful about feeding them and buying the correct seeds. The result is that we have all kinds of species, and also a very acrobatic squirrel. They are not always harmonious with each other, and Elgar does his utmost to scatter the pigeons. He is mesmerised by them, but they can fly, and he cannot.

The good news is that the swallows are back. They flit about, finding insects for their young. What a pleasure to see them and to listen to them twittering. But I have a guilty secret, which I must get off my chest. It was when I had my old MG car, and the swallows had just arrived. They decided that they would like to make their nest in my new carport. What fun they had in there. My lovely car was systematically being destroyed. I watched in despair.

It became a competition: the swallows would go back and forth, carefully assembling their nests, while I dismantled them daily. I hated myself for doing this, and I still feel guilty about it whenever I think about what I did, but it was them or me. As fast as they attempted to build, I dismantled daily. Eventually the swallows gave up and found pastures new. Ten years later they are back and I could weep with joy. I could never forgive myself for what I did. I no longer use the car – I no longer drive. And what a pleasure it is, watching the busy birds making their home tirelessly; and I guard them with my life.

All the birds are nesting at the moment, and Chris points out a bullfinch to me. We go through the usual rigmarole: where is it, I can't see it, I tell him. It's there, in the far corner he tells me, guiding my head; and for a split second I can see it. A bright patch of red on its chest. A second afterwards it has vanished. Is it still there? I ask him and he confirms that it is. But I cannot see it, despite squinting. I can no longer locate the whereabouts of the bird. How sad.

FORTY – NOT ONE OR THE OTHER

I have been pondering over something: given my situation, I have been wondering whether it would be preferable to have my cognitive function intact, whereby I understand everything that is happening to me and am able to join in a conversation, or, whether life would be easier if I was blissfully unaware of what was going on around me.

On balance I think it is preferable to have PCA rather than the more usual form of Alzheimer's. But of course, there are many variants with Alzheimer's and everyone will have their own experiences, and own story. With PCA the essence, that is me, is more or less unimpaired, so my comparison is a futile exercise. Recently there has been an exciting breakthrough, and it was announced that a cure for Alzheimer's is possibly close; this is, of course, marvellous news; it is too late for myself, but hopefully it will benefit others.

Anyway, meanwhile, I can hardly contain my excitement: my brother, who lives in Tel Aviv is coming over to see me in a few days' time. We have not seen one another for more than a year, and we are very close. Under normal circumstances we would see each other three or four times a year, but these are not normal times. Will he notice the changes in me? Will I notice the changes in him? He has Parkinson's, and was diagnosed at a similar time with his illness as I was with mine. We are very alike in many ways; we share a similar outlook on life, and try not to take ourselves too seriously. I miss him hugely when he goes back to Israel, and worry about the situation there: and the less said about that, the better; however, there are faults on both sides and suffice to say, I wish I could bang their heads together.

By coincidence, also, he will be visiting a friend of his while in England, who also has Alzheimer's, and I shall be meeting him. It will be interesting to compare notes, as it were. Will he be further down the line than myself, or maybe we will be on a par with one another, but this all conjecture. There are so many different forms of Alzheimer's.

I have three mottos in life: the first one is, smile and the world smiles with you; the second is, at all times have a sense of humour. And the third aphorism, which I particularly like is: people who mind, don't matter; people who matter don't mind.

This morning did not begin well. I had woken too early, and could not return to sleep. I was overly excited about seeing my brother again after so long, but by the same token I was anxious. As usual, Elgar and myself went for a walk. It was cold for the time of year, and I couldn't stop shivering. I longed to get home as I was freezing. I slipped on Elgar's lead to hurry him up, as he was stopping to sniff at everything in sight. I think that must have been when it happened: I had been walking without a thought, when I realised that yet again I had taken a wrong turn. This was becoming a habit. And I suddenly felt afraid. People would start to think of me as that batty woman who gets lost all the time. I realised that my Alzheimer's had taken a new turn. And then I saw a tall figure: the figure resembled Chris, but it could not be him as he had walked into town, and this was in a completely different direction. I squinted then, and the tall man smiled at me. And I realised then, of course it was indeed my husband. In the past, he had teased me about not recognising him. To be fair, there are quite a few tall, silver-haired men in the locality. I was so upset, I was mortified and heartbroken – everything combined. How could I not recognise my lovely husband? And I wept and could not stop weeping for several hours.

I feel now that I have reached a turning point with my illness. I watch my own disintegration, and it is horrible.

And now I shall revert to my brother's longed for visit. We had regularly spoken on, FaceTime, but it was a poor substitute for seeing him in reality. I had been worried that I would find him changed; that his Parkinson's might have further deteriorated; but when it came to seeing him again, in actuality, it was not the case: he was my same big brother, that I had always loved, with the same irreverent humour, the same silly jokes, the same giggle, the same stubbornness, and the same boy who had mercilessly teased me when he was a child. I fell into his arms in relief.

The first day of his visit we spent catching up. For his second day, he had arranged a party for his old friends, whom he had known since childhood. In all, we were thirteen people, and I knew nearly everyone there. The restaurant where the party was to take place was also familiar to me, so I felt none of the usual anxiety which afflicts me when I am stressed.

A man whom I did not know approached me, and introduced himself by name.

"Hello, I'm Ben," he announced, with a firm handshake.
"And whom might you be?" He added,
with a twinkle in his eye.

I laughed, and told him my name.

"We are lucky with the weather," he commented. He
paused for a moment and after a second or two, said
again, "I'm Ben, it's nice weather isn't it." He paused yet
again. Then almost immediately repeated,
"And whom might you be?"

I realised that this was my brother's friend,
who had Alzheimer's.

His wife, a doctor, then came up to me and the three
of us sat together for a while. It was difficult to extract
a meaningful conversation from him, but his wife did her
utmost to include him in what was being said, and to
explain what was going on. He nodded as though he was
totally in control of his faculties, but I realised he had very
little comprehension of what was being said and repeatedly
interjected with the refrain, "I am Ben, and who are you?"
Sometimes I would detect, in his eyes a sadness, and he
would turn to his wife for reassurance.

Later that day, when the party guests had left, my brother
explained that Ben used to be a top lawyer.

Now I can answer my own question as to whether I would
rather have PCA as my enemy, or the more usual form of
Alzheimer's such as I have just described. The answer is,
I would rather be as I am, for as long as I can.

FORTY-ONE – WORKING WITH ALZHEIMER'S RESEARCH, UK

It is a dull Monday afternoon—when isn't it? My brother had left the day before, and I was already missing him. He had rung earlier for a chat and to talk about when we might get together again, when minutes later, the phone rang again. I picked it up, thinking it might be him and I smiled in readiness.

The voice at the other end asked,
"Am I speaking to Valerie Blumenthal?"

"Yes, you are," I affirmed,
swallowing my disappointment that it was not my brother.

It transpired that the caller was from Alzheimer's Research, UK. For several years I'd assisted them with various projects, and consequently they had bestowed on me the grand title of a Champion Volunteer!

For a few minutes we chatted generally, then she explained the purpose of the call: and for this I think it would be logical to enclose the email that she had sent to me, on behalf of Alzheimer's Research, UK, so here it is:

From: Jude Clarke
To: Valerie Blumenthal
Subject: Inspirational poster at Head Office

Good morning,
I have what I hope is a quite nice request.

At ARUK we are making plans to get back into the office again, after a long period when most of us have been working from home.

Ahead of this, our Brand team are organising a "refresh" of the office décor. As part of this they asked my team to suggest some of our Champions and Media and Comms volunteers who they could use, with a photo and an inspirational quote, to make a poster for around the office.

With your permission, we would love to use you, as an inspiring reminder of the people on whose behalf we are all working so hard for.

The wording that I have identified, from previous conversations with you, is:

"I'd be thrilled if others could learn from my situation. I try to focus on what I can do rather than what I can't. What I wish, more than anything, is that everyone could be made aware of this illness. Knowledge of it could prevent so much anguish."

Would you be OK for us to use this, alongside one of these lovely pictures of you (attached)?

Thanks so much for your support,

All the best

Jude

And here was my reply:

Thank you so much. I feel very honoured and if it does some good, that is all that matters. Well done for all your hard work, and of course I give my permission.

Writing this has prompted me to recall my Singalong, which I organised for Alzheimer's Research UK, about six or seven years ago – I cannot remember exactly how long ago it was – but by now you'll be used to my hazy memory! The idea for the Singalong had come to me in the middle of the night. The more I thought about it, the more my excitement grew. One minute I would chastise myself for thinking I would be capable of doing something so ambitious; the next, a voice would interrupt, you can, you can.

The first thing was to tell everybody in the village about the Singalong. I also told members of Alzheimer's Research UK of my plans. There was no excuse now not to go ahead.

Hee, hee, hee, laughed the Brain Gremlins, anticipating my humiliation. Fortunately, I had kept all the musical arrangements I had painstakingly put together, from when I had my choir.

The day itself loomed – bitterly cold for an early April day. The event was to be held in a neighbour's barn, and I had issued instructions for everyone to arrive promptly. I was, understandably, very nervous but, by the same token, I felt energised. A member of Alzheimer's Research UK had brought collection buckets and display banners.

People began to arrive: a depressing a trickle at first, so that I feared the whole thing would be a disaster. But then, a large group of people arrived simultaneously and the barn was filled with chatting and laughing. Chris was kept busy handing out the song sheets, which I had prepared.

I welcomed everybody, and, looking around the packed room, thanked them for their support. Following this, the representative from ARUK gave a short address. And then the singing started in earnest.

To get everyone into the right frame of mood we began with a sea shanty. I divided the singers into male and female, which worked perfectly as the numbers were nearly equal.

What shall we do with the Drunken Sailor, rang out the lusty sea shanty, amidst much hilarity.

This opener created a relaxed atmosphere. We then became more ambitious and other songs that we sang included *Summertime*, *Blowing in The Wind* and *All My Trials*. These were all in three parts.

As the day drew to an end, I remember feeling euphoric. Best of all, we had raised a thousand pounds, thanks to everyone's generosity.

I wish I could do it again. Sometimes I think perhaps I could, but in all honesty I don't think I would be able to.

FORTY-TWO – PAINTING

Tentative, I pick up the paintbrush that quivers
in my shaky fingers.

I feel excited. It is nearly a year since I have done any
painting, and I have been using every possible excuse
to avoid it, because I thought I would be disappointed.
And I was; I am. However, I am determined to find a way.
There must be a way. In the past, I used acrylics or oil.
I painted literally, and had joined a group of others for life
drawing. When my PCA became apparent, I was baffled
by what was happening to me. I could not understand
why my painting had become increasingly difficult.

My PCA went through stages, regarding painting. The first
stage was looser than it had been and was, you could say,
almost expressionist; but as the years have passed my work
has become more abstract. However, until comparatively
recently, I was still able to draw recognisable figures.

I loved laying out the materials that I would need, and
selecting my colours and brushes; but then I became more
and more muddled, and was unable to recognise what was
what. I knew I would have to completely change my style.
It was a radical decision but one I realised I would have to
take. I had heard of oil pastels, but never used them. Now
was my chance to try. Using oil pastels has meant that at
least I don't have lots of little bits to deal with. I can now
use my fingers for much of what I am trying to convey;
however, I am limited by what I can paint and that annoys
me. I find myself confined to painting nature. There again,
surely nature is infinite with its possibilities. What is good

about oil pastels is that the results are instant.
This is ideal for someone as impatient as myself.

It is nearly a year since I last tried to paint. Like everyone
else during the pandemic, I have felt lethargic and
uninspired; also I suffer from cold and my room where
I work is always chilly. But here I am now, on this summer's
day, poised, ready to take that first step, and it is ridiculous
how nervous I am. The first colour I pick out, is an Azure
blue; the colour of the sky, beautiful and gentle. It reminds
me of lovely Portscatho, in Cornwall. I first discovered
Portscatho more than 20 years ago. I remember there was
an old-fashioned hairdresser's, with two big round driers
that looked like hats that encompassed your head. Hair
took for ever to dry, and smelt of perms. Those days have
long gone, but there is still a thriving community, and a
village store which caters for most essentials.

In six weeks' time, this little place is where you will find us.
And yes, of course it has changed over the years that we
have known it, but on the whole it is still unspoiled. We will
be going in early September when the school holidays are
over with, and the hordes have disappeared. Every year
I vow that I will swim in the sea. However, in reality I have
only twice done that, as it has been too cold. This year
I shall; I am determined to do so. And my friend who lives
there will accompany me.

We rent the same cottage every year, which makes life
much easier for me; I know my way around it, as does the
dog. Also, we have made several friends there, over the
years. I am able to picture it clearly: it is only a few metres
from a sandy beach, and out of season, dogs are allowed.

Stone steps lead to the harbour where fishing boats rock gently to and fro, to and fro, creaking in unison. Bold children jump from the jetty, with delighted squeals, and I can only envy them.

And I shall take the more sedate route, via the slipway, and pick my way tentatively towards the sea. In my mind's eye, I am envisaging the entire scene and wish I could fast forward my daydreaming.

I am quite pleased with the sky that I have created, although, perhaps it is a little bland. And now I become more adventurous and I select a Prussian Blue. Unfortunately, I splodge this and have to disguise it somehow. Just the job: I shall do a large bird. A red kite would be perfect. In fact, I shall do two, for good measure. I had intended them to be red kites, but they could be anything really, and they are rather wobbly! Picasso I am not, but I have passed a very pleasant afternoon.
And through the window, outside, I can see my husband picking courgettes that he has grown himself, and which are intended for tonight's meal.

There is a postscript.

A couple of months after writing this, there was an art exhibition in the village, and a total stranger noticed two of my paintings. He asked whether they were for sale. I was stunned; I wanted to burst out laughing, but I kept a straight face as he eulogised over my loose painting technique and use of colours. I walked away with a hundred and fifty pounds and a sense of pride.

FORTY-THREE – PUT AWAY CHILDISH THINGS

Every so often, over the years, I am assaulted by a
memory. Unbidden, it comes into my head, entering my
consciousness with renewed shock; it never quite leaves
me. I have been debating whether or not to include
this in my book.

I was about eight years old at the time. Perhaps I should
put the situation into context. I had an idyllic childhood –
I want that to be made clear. I grew up in West Hampstead,
on the edge of Cricklewood in London. From there it was
an easy walk to Golders Hill Park, where you could see a
variety of animals: deer, sheep, exotic chickens, and goats.
The goats were my favourites. They were very friendly.
They used to come right up to you and snuffle round
you. You were not supposed to give them food. There
was a large notice warning you of this, but of course we
children disobeyed. It was a lovely part of London, with a
rural feel to it and wild areas. In summer amateur artists
would exhibit their paintings and ceramics and everything
seemed so bright and happy, and we children were treated
to ice creams and donkey rides.

We would run around freely, outside, while our parents
and their friends were in the Bull and Bush – and,
as I write this, I have only just remembered about the
Bull and Bush, which was one of the most famous pubs
in Hampstead. I remember the sound of grown-up
laughter coming from inside; the jovial laughter,
which somehow made you feel safe.

A little further on was Hampstead, where I learnt to ride. I remember that the teacher was very strict, and I was terrified of her; she seemed very old to me, but in reality she was probably about twenty. I had the same pony to ride each time, and it was a stubborn creature – lazy and bad-tempered. Poor thing, it must have had such a boring, monotonous life; but as a child I would have not thought about it. Childhood seemed to sparkle and be full of mysteries and hope.

We were a happy little gang, all living in the same road, or neighbouring ones, and we were in and out of each other's homes. School was a mile or so away, and often I would walk with my friend Jane and her sister, Susie. Sometimes, on the way back, I would take a shortcut through the cemetery with all its silent gravestones leering at me. It was a spooky place for a young child who had a vivid imagination, and I would always scuttle past, hurriedly. I imagined ghostly figures taunting me and laughing at me. As for school itself, I loathed school. I was not academic in any shape or form and I would daydream the tedious hours away. My dyspraxia would not have been recognised in those days and I was always being reprimanded for laziness.

My singing saved me. I had been blessed with an operatic voice from a young age. The result of this was that the teachers were more lenient than they might have been.

My parents were quite strict with us, more so with me than my brother, nonetheless, the house was full of love, and laughter. I remember little details: the whirring of my mother's sewing machine, which was always in use; she loved sewing and making clothes for us. I remember her re-upholstering a chair; it was quite an undertaking, because of its size. I kept it for years, but only a few months ago I noticed that the mice had been at it and nibbled it beyond repair. I remember how my mother loved flowers and flower arranging; her home meant everything to her, and she thought only of us and our well-being.

Our house was an old-fashioned, three-storey building that took a lot of cleaning, and my mother was endlessly busy, in addition, she chaired an important charity, which took up much of her time. My parents took on a husband and wife team to live in; he would do the gardening and be a general handyman, while his wife would do the housework and cooking. The pair were Italian and after a year or so, Lorenzo and Josephine had become trusted members of the family. I often used to go and sit with them in their room, in the evening. By the age of eight I could speak reasonable Italian. Lorenzo would tease me. It was funny at first, but then he started the game of tickle. He did this openly, and my parents seemed to think it was amusing. I found it annoying, and would protest.

My parents took long holidays abroad. I cannot remember the subsequent order of events which then took place. I remember that it was dark. I was curled up, asleep, and I remember movement in the room. What I do know is, Lorenzo suddenly appeared in my bedroom. I was about eight at the time, and I remember that fact, because I slept with a particular doll which had beautiful long hair. I remember being surprised that he was in my bedroom, but I was not afraid; I knew him well, therefore why should I feel worried? I remember him talking to me softly, in

Italian, and then a strange sensation between my legs. He had woken me from a deep sleep, and I was still only half awake. I remember his voice saying "Is that nice?" then I remember silence, and he tiptoed away. I did not understand what had happened, and I fell back to sleep. It happened on three more occasions, and I sensed it was not right; I sensed that what he was doing was bad. It felt wrong, and I wanted him never to touch me again. In my polite little voice, I told him, "Lorenzo, I don't want you to come into my room anymore." And subsequently he made no attempt to molest me again. I have never understood how he was able to come into my bedroom without being seen or heard, or without his wife knowing.

For many years, I told no-one about what had happened. I cannot say truthfully that I had been traumatised by what had taken place, but after that, I avoided Lorenzo as far as I was able to. Not long after this, the couple left, and I returned to being a child. Many years passed, and finally I told my parents what had taken place. Their reactions surprised me. They were disbelieving. My mother went silent, whilst my father refused to believe it could have happened, despite my insistence that it was the truth. He changed the subject and it was never raised again. It was a different era in those days.

Whilst the events have not changed me as a person and nor has my life been ruined, they could have easily done so; and I am so angry now, thinking about it. How dare he? I am indignant and enraged on behalf of the child I was.

Lorenzo would be long gone by now, but I wonder how many other children he had abused during his life.

FORTY-FOUR – THE VILLAGE PARTY

Yesterday was the village party. Naturally, it rained.
For once the forecast was correct. One by one, people
had been cancelling with lame excuses, however, despite
that, we ended up with about twenty people – quite
a respectable number, considering. As usual, I was
nervous, even though I knew almost everyone there.

Chris and I had made a cake together and, as usual,
there was a squabble. It was about how many eggs were
required, what should go in first, et cetera, et cetera. It's
my recipe, I told my husband. Yes, that may be, he said,
but you can't see what you are doing. The eggs have to
go in first, I explained, becoming heated. It says here, that
the sugar should go in, he insisted, and that stubborn look
came into his eyes and I knew that there would be
a protracted argument, which did not bode well.

Do it yourself then, he said. But I can't do it without you,
I said, hearing my voice sounding plaintive.

Eventually, a cake somehow got made.

You've got chocolate all over your mouth, he said. As we
were about to leave for the party, fuming I washed my face,
and re-did my make-up. I reminded myself that it was not
his fault because he was a Capricorn, and Capricorns are
known to be stubborn.

I wish I didn't become so nervous before parties, but
I cannot help myself. I would like to bring back the old
me. I feel that everyone must be comparing that other

person who I used to be to the current me. I imagine them discussing me and feeling sorry for me, and so, to compensate, I make jokes and attempt to be witty. I make sure that I look good and that nothing is out of place with my appearance, but it is becoming increasingly difficult, and it is such an effort.

I am conscious of walking strangely, and this is because of my vision. I have to be so careful that I do not fall; life is full of unexpected hazards for me. We have lovely friends, who have a magnificent garden, with water features and secret paths and steps, but it is like negotiating the famous steps in Gibraltar. I am petrified when I go to their lovely home. People are so kind, and I can tell that they really care about me. It is me that I do not like, and that is the truth.

Our village is small, and everyone at the party knows me. I feel that they are sad to see me as I am now. Everyone rushes towards me, which is so kind, and I really am grateful, but it only emphasises the changes within me. I do not want to harp on about myself, but I have to be realistic as I write this. I am very aware now that my illness is becoming much, much worse. I can longer hide this, and sometimes I have bad thoughts which I cannot always banish. I am sure that this must be normal and I do not want to give in to it. I feel so bad that I have constantly to leave so much to Chris. I hear my voice calling out again, Chris, can you help me? And he must sometimes dread my voice. But now I feel myself becoming self-pitying and that is the last thing I want.

FORTY-FIVE – END OF AN ERA

Like everybody else at the moment, I have been glued to the Olympics, in particular, the dressage and three-day eventing. I realise I have, earlier, written about my horse, Fleetwood, and naturally, the Olympics has brought back memories of him and our many years together.

The day before Fleetwood died, I dreamt of his death. It was uncanny: in my dream, my horse was dying, and he was unable to move. The other horses in the field were all crowding around him, as though they understood that something was very wrong. I awoke from my dream in tears. The following day, in reality, that is exactly what occurred. These coincidences do seem very strange indeed. I do often seem to have premonitions. There was no pain, I could tell that. He even tried to chomp on an apple. But he just could not, despite the encouragement of his friends, who kept nuzzling him. And, as in my dream, I stood helpless, soothing him, realising he was dying on his feet, in his old age.

The vet arrived after half an hour or so. He administered a painless injection of morphine and, with me stroking him, my wonderful horse went down on his knees then rolled into peaceful sleep.

As I write this, so the memories flood back anew. I still feel the power of him beneath my feet, his eagerness as he broke into a canter, and I can envisage his beautiful eyes. And how, when we practised our dressage, he would obey my directions and move as if we were one.

I was bereft without my companion. I even missed the mucking out, and the husbandry involved with having a horse to look after. I missed the little wicker of pleasure that he gave me when he saw me approach.

For as long as I can remember, I had a horse. I rode for the sheer love of it, always with my German Shepherd who kept pace with us, alongside. I did not hunt; I have no desire to kill another creature. I rode for the joy of it. Why should I want to kill a beautiful animal and label it as sport? I simply cannot comprehend why anyone would want to harm another living creature.

It so happened that in the field where I had used to keep Fleetwood, the farmer had acquired an ex-racehorse. He was a stunning animal--like a Stubbs painting, and very tall, with fine features. Excitedly, I took him on. However, Remo, as he was called, was highly strung, and as well as being stubborn, he would try to buck me off, if he did not want to do as I wanted.

I completely lost my nerve when, one day, I just missed having a very bad accident. I re-homed him to a well-known jockey, who was more experienced than myself with racehorses. I have to say it was a relief, but nonetheless, I felt a failure, and also I was sad as Remo's temperament was very gentle and I missed him.

And so, to Henry! Yes, who would have guessed that one day I would end up having a Shire horse? Henry was advertised as a Shire cross and, duly, I drove nearly a hundred miles to see him. After a cup of tea and a lengthy chit-chat, by which time I was becoming impatient, the horse was led out from the yard. My first reaction was to gasp, my next was to laugh. I knew enough about horses to recognise that this was a full blown Shire horse, with nothing else in the mix. The immense beast that stood proudly in front of me was approaching seventeen hands. I was barely eight stone. Without a doubt, he was a magnificent animal. I was still agile in those days, but it occurred to me that mounting the horse might present a challenge. I stroked his great head, and in return received a nudge of affection. What could I do? At that point, I fell in love.

On a wet day, I took delivery of him.

"What do you want with a cart horse?" The man who delivered Henry demanded, as Henry tottered out tentatively from the horsebox.

"He is not a carthorse," I retorted. "He is a Shire horse." Putting him straight in a stern tone.

"What's the difference?" The man demanded.

"He is an ancient breed," I explained.

He shrugged, and murmured something about meat. I ignored him. He clearly thought he was funny.

When he had departed I led Henry into his large stable and made him comfortable; he immediately chomped on hay and horse nuts.

That night there was a ferocious storm. Thunder raged, and as Henry paced up and down in distress, lightning lit up the stable and Henry's eyes rolled in terror. I did my utmost to soothe him and kept a tight grip on him, trying to sound calm, trying not to let him see my own fear. I was worried that he would trample on me with his immense strength. My German Shepherd was with me also, and that seemed to placate him. Henry became calm and the storm passed without mishap; I could tell that he trusted me. But it was quite an induction.

Henry and I struck up a strong bond over the years but he had his issues. He was what is known as cold backed. This is when a horse puffs itself out when it is about to be ridden. This makes it impossible to mount the animal and to buckle up the girth, as it has swollen itself to such an extent. Little by little this disperses, along with the tension. The first time this happened I was shaken, as Henry tore around the paddock, farting and releasing painful wind. I was disconcerted, to say the least, but as soon as I understood the phenomenon, I just left him for a few minutes until the painful wind dispersed. It was rather like having to wind a giant baby!

Strange habits aside, Henry was a fantastic horse in every way. Despite his bulk, he could canter and gallop with the best of them. He restored my confidence, and everyone stopped to watch as we passed sedately through the village.

Riding Henry was like sitting on a soft warm cushion, one which I knew would keep me safe, and that I could rely on. Even his name sounded dependable and it fitted him to a tee. However, as the years went by, I was having trouble with my hips, and Henry's great weight was not helping matters. I tried to ignore my discomfort as far as I was able, but it was not long before every step I took was torture and pierced through my groin. When I could no longer stand the pain, I had no option but to pay a visit to the doctor. A scan was recommended, and a week later I was summoned to the surgeon's consulting room.

With my fingers crossed for good luck, I went into the room. Please, please, I prayed silently, but I knew that God was not listening.

I should have made a note of the day: it was Thursday. Historically, Thursdays have always been a bad day for me. I was burgled on a Thursday, my cat was run over on a Thursday, Richard, my previous partner died on a Thursday and, more recently, my father died on Thursday; as a schoolgirl we always had double maths on a Thursday. I hated maths. It was my worst subject and always remained so. However, I took none of these issues into consideration as I made arrangements for my time in hospital. Over the years, Chris and I had rekindled our relationship, and he drove me to the hospital. All I wanted was to rid myself of the awful pain.

I woke up from the anaesthetic in a bewildered fog. I knew straightaway that something was very wrong. I could not feel my leg at all. It was completely numb, and without any sensation. I rang for the nurse, who assured me that everything was fine; nonetheless, I was still uneasy. A day later I could still feel nothing, and likewise, the day after that. I told the sister about my fears.

"You're being too impatient," she said, not even trying to hide her exasperation. And I could feel the panic rising within me. Why would no one believe me?

When it was time to leave the hospital I was afraid and in tears. Finally, I was sent for a scan and the results showed that I had 90% paralysis in my leg. My femoral nerve had been almost severed.

I am not going to dwell any further on this subject for two reasons: one is I have no desire to bore anyone who might be reading this, the second is because, quite honestly, it is too painful for me to relive that whole period. I will simply say that I lost a year of my life. I should also say that I never rode a horse again.

As for wonderful Henry, I had retired him and he was very happy in his field for several years more. The day came when another horse was introduced into the adjacent field, and the two horses used to whinny to each other. Then one day a neighbour rang to say that Henry was lying down and not moving. I ran to the field, with Chris, and there he was. He was no longer in his own field but must have barged his way through the fence, and doubtless, the pair of them would have galloped about together. However, the other horse was an athletic thoroughbred and Henry was – well, Henry. It was not difficult to put two and two together as to what had happened. Henry would have had a heart attack, and died on the spot. A friend of mine who was a horse vet, said he would have not have suffered, and that it would have been a wonderful way for a horse to go.

To finish this piece, I would like to remember my father. It had been he who had bought Henry for me, and he had always had a soft spot for him.

A RANDOM JOTTING

Sometimes, in my imagination I can see the sea. Sometimes I can taste fresh soil, and it is beautiful and I want to dig my nails into it. And sometimes I feel as though I am a circular and I am at one with nature. I am nature. A pastiche of the past – floating back, in no particular order.

FORTY-SIX – MY BIRTHDAY

Today is my birthday; don't ask me my age. Suffice to
say that a lot of years have passed since I was born.
A clue: I have an eleven year-old granddaughter, and my
own daughter is approaching a landmark birthday. How
on earth could I have accumulated so many years; good,
bad, indifferent, memorable. All the highlights; all the
excitement; all the beauty; all the laughter; all the joy
and sorrow. In other words, all these things make up the
marvellous mix of life.

And what then? Is there another beginning, after the
end? I hope there is. I really hope there is. I am scared of
nothingness. Ever since childhood I have been afraid of
nothingness. But at this moment my mind is full of joy.
Life is beautiful and I shall cherish it, with all its flaws.

I awoke early this morning in anticipation. Chris has
laid out my birthday cards with his in the centre.
We read that together, first. As usual his card is full
of love and deep meaning. I have had a dozen other
cards from friends and family, and was so touched
that they had remembered my birthday.

Chris helps me to get dressed. I dab on the Chanel
perfume which is his gift to me. In the evening we will
be going to a smart restaurant to celebrate. Meanwhile,
the phone does not stop ringing. I am so touched.
How lucky I am to have such loyal friends.

FORTY-SEVEN – RUBY

And now, I think it is time I talk about Ruby.
Oh, my lovely Ruby.

You used to come and stay with us quite often. We had
such fun, at least, I hope you think we did. You called
me Granma V. And for a treat we would sometimes go
to Tiggywinkles, which is an animal rescue sanctuary –
primarily it is for hedgehogs, though there is usually an
assortment of other animals and birds also.

We went on lovely walks, just me and you. Sometimes you
would get a little bored and I would make up stories. We
would find wild flowers, and press them in a book when
we returned home. In those days, my German Shepherd
dog, Mozart, was with us, and you loved him. I can picture
you so clearly as a little girl, and now look at you! At that
time, you always had to have a story, of course. The more
frightening, the better; in the story, Mozart would always
come to the rescue just in time.

I made up a special song: it went like this:

> *Bubbles and puddles are fun, boom, boom,*
> *Bubbles and cuddles are fun, boom, boom,*
> *Paddle and poddle in big fat puddles,*
> *Oh, puddles and poddles are fun.*

Soon you will be going to a new school where you will be
embarking on a new and exciting era.

Be happy, my Darling.

FORTY-EIGHT – A BUCOLIC LANDSCAPE

"I don't think it's for you," the estate agent told me in a firm tone, as the thatched cottage came into view. When I first set eyes on Vine Cottage, nestled by itself in the conservation area of the village, I literally went weak at the knees. Thirty years later, I asked the estate agent – who had become a friend – why she had made that remark.

"I thought you would want something grander," came her reply.

"But I'm not grand," I protested.

"I know that now," she said.

It is August, and at last the weather is behaving appropriately for the time of year. The Red Kites have been cycling joyfully for the last ten minutes. Chris is mowing the lawn, up and down he goes in a mindless rhythm. I used to enjoy mowing the lawn, but that was a long time ago, and now I would more than likely cut off my toes. But the sound is comforting, nonetheless. Homely. All is well with the world, it seems to say. (I wish it was.) And at the far end of the garden, I suddenly realise, the sunflowers have come out. How I love sunflowers, they have such happy smiles.

I take a tour of the garden: about three quarters of an acre in all. To my gratification I can see baby grapes forming on the vine. They are definitely growing bigger, and seem very healthy. This little sign of burgeoning life fills me with a deep pleasure. I had been worried that, because of the unseasonal weather, they would wither and die, but like

valiant soldiers they have triumphed, despite the odds.
In another month or so, they will have turned a midnight
blue and will be ready to eat; in my mind,
I can almost taste them.

It was time for my second walk of the day with Elgar.
I was wary, the reason being that the burdock thistles
were at their peak. These horrible things have a nasty
habit of attaching themselves to everything that brushes
past them. This happened to Elgar only a week ago, and
he was covered in the sticky balls, which are almost the
size of golf balls. He was distraught and it took me almost
two hours to disentangle them from his thick coat. He was
so good; clearly, he knew that I was trying to help him.
Anyway, to return to my walk I was, understandably,
ultra-cautious and left his lead on him.

As I drew closer to the field I could hear the mournful
baying of cows, and their chomping sounds, as they
greedily grazed. There must have been thirty cattle in the
field, and a huge bull ruled supreme. What a magnificent
beast he was. It occurred to me that the scene was like a
Constable painting. I stood there, staring at the scene for
ages. I wished I could have photographed it. Elgar stayed
close to me all the while and I could almost feel his relief
when we turned to go home.

FORTY-NINE – WITCH

Now I am going to go off piste, as it were! What I am about to tell you started approximately forty years ago. Saying that, it seems extraordinary that so many years have passed, and I have to say that number out loud again in order to make it real. A friend of mine – I shall call him Ben for privacy – was in severe pain due to a ligament problem in his hand. It had been troubling him for months and he was due to have an operation in ten days' time. We were discussing the situation when I felt a strange and inexplicable sensation within myself; it was as if my hand was gravitating towards his hand, almost like a magnet.

"Can we just try something?" I asked him.

"What do you mean?" He asked.

"I don't know," I replied, "but I have a compulsion to put my hand on top of yours. It's as though it is pushing me to do so," I told him.

Gently, I took hold of his hand and laid mine on his; there it was again, that same magnetic sensation. It was as though our hands were co-joined, like twins. I could no longer differentiate my hand from Ben's. After a minute I slowly moved my hand from his. Ben wiggled his fingers about.

He stared at me in astonishment. "Doesn't hurt so much," he told me. "In fact, it doesn't hurt at all."

"We mustn't get our hopes up," I told him, cautiously. "It may just be a fluke."

"The pain is bound to come back," Ben said gloomily.

For the next three days I repeated the same procedure. Each time there was the same reaction. My fingers would tingle for several minutes afterwards. What was even stranger, only my little finger seemed to have an effect: It was this finger which was misshapen when, as a child I had damaged it in the car door.

After seven days, the specialist declared that there was no sign of any problem with the ligament.

Ben cancelled the appointment that he had made.

It was a few weeks later, and friend of mine had come round, she was in agony with sciatica and was almost in tears.

I hesitated, "Would you let me try something," I asked her. "It may or may not work." I could already feel my fingers seaming to tingle, in particular my middle finger. I placed my hand on her back. I could feel my little finger beginning to throb as though in anticipation.

"What are you doing," my friend asked.

"I don't know," I replied, "I really don't know," I said again, "but it seems to work." I positioned my little finger where I gauged the pain to be and gently applied pressure there. Within a couple of minutes I could feel that it was working and I kept my hand in the same position for a while. It is very hard to explain, that sensation and that tingling, which is almost like a series of small electric shocks. I released my hand from hers.

"The pain has gone," my friend informed me, in a disbelieving tone and repeated, "it has completely gone. You are a witch," she went on, laughing, "a bloody witch. In another era you would be burnt at the stake."

My next candidate was my German Shepherd, Brahms. I was in St Ives, on holiday, and, as with all my dogs that I have had, he was with me also. It was late evening, and Brahms was asleep on his rug, flat out after his day of swimming. One of his legs was dangling in a relaxed pose, and I rubbed his tummy. In response he rolled onto his stomach, I noticed then he had a growth under his arm. Alarmed, I stared at it. It was the size of a walnut. The next day I drove to the vet, having asked for directions beforehand. I drove around and around the narrow winding lanes, getting more and more lost. After much frustration I finally found it down a tiny side road.

"I'm so sorry," I began.

The vet waved his hand dismissively.

"Worry not," he said cheerfully.
"Everyone gets lost coming here. He looked at Brahms, and commented "He's a big chap isn't he.
So what is the problem with him?" He queried.

I explained the situation to him and the Vet examined Brahms carefully.

"It's a Lipoma," he explained. "It's quite common, and it's almost certainly benign, but because of its position near his underarm, you will probably need to have it removed, as it will chafe and he will be uncomfortable. When you get back home you will need to speak to your vet."

"Could it just go by itself," I asked him.

He shook his head emphatically.
"No," he replied, "you will need to have it taken off."

I drove back to the B & B, where I was staying, feeling reassured. An idea came to suddenly. What if I were to try laying my hands on Brahms? Tentatively, lovingly, I did so. Almost immediately I was conscious of that tingling sensation, throbbing in my little finger. Brahms seemed to be almost in a trance, and his eyes closed. Twice a day, for three days, I repeated this procedure; on the third I realised that extraordinarily, the growth had substantially reduced. On the remaining days left to us it continued to shrink. By the time we arrived home, there was almost no trace of it, and after further couple of days there was nothing to see at all. It showed no trace of ever having existed.

Back home, I went to my own Vet, and explained, trying not to sound ridiculous, the whole saga.

"Could it have gone on its own," I asked?

"No, definitely not," he replied and with a smile, he added, "you must be some kind of witch."

Over the years I have had many such experiences. I cannot explain them. I can only assume that it is some kind of energy within me. It does not always work, but usually it does. I tell hardly anyone about this strange phenomena, indeed, I feel embarrassed to mention it.

I just wish I could heal myself.

FIFTY – PORTSCATHO

Where has summer gone? Today must surely rank as one of the coldest Augusts on record. I am wearing all my warmest winter clothes, and still I am freezing. Oh, bring back hot flushes. I hanker for a glorious summers' day, where everything is yellow, instead of sludge grey. And now I have a dilemma: I have been longing to return to Portscatho, in Cornwall; however, the bitterly cold weather is hardly conducive to sunbathing, and besides that, I am not one of nature's stoic individuals. One minute I think we should cancel Portscatho, the next I think that we would regret doing so. Chris is leaving the decision to me. I have other anxieties as well: will I be able to tackle the steep steps which lead to the beach? Just thinking about them makes me feel jittery. Oh, but it is so beautiful. I can picture it now, and I can picture the bench seat where we always sit and watch the sun go down, in the early evening. Chris will be sketching the scene on his pad, whilst I would just gaze out to sea, taking it all in. I phoned my friend who lives there. She always has good advice to impart.

"You may as well go, as you've paid anyway," she said. "I would love to see you of course, but it's up to you," she finished. "It has to be your decision," she added. So still I was none the wiser.

I pictured myself in the little living room of the rented cottage. It would be cold; the central heating was, at best, tepid and the bathroom was cramped. You're being pathetic, I told myself, those are not reasons to cry off. Then a different image presented itself to me; and, now I was in The Feathers pub, chatting to friends, whom we had not seen for a year or so. I could almost taste the sea, and I imagined the seagulls greedily stealing food from unsuspecting holiday makers. My mind is made up.

"We have to go," I tell Chris.
"We can't not go to Portscatho."

And as I spoke, I felt a sense of relief within me, and a lightness of being. I rang up my friend again.

"It's on," I told her, hardly able to contain my excitement.
"We'll see you in a weeks' time –
with swimming costumes."

It was just two days later. A lot can happen in two days. Ever cautious, we had been listening to the news. The number of Covid cases had been rising alarmingly, particularly throughout Cornwall. With sinking heart, I rang my friend yet again. She confirmed that the number of cases in Portscatho had already shot up, and would increase still further over the Bank Holiday and Regatta weekend.

"The restaurant and pub will be packed," my friend told me. "And you know how you hate crowds. Quite honestly, I've never seen Portscatho so busy. I would advise you not to come. We are just going to hide ourselves away."

So that is that.

I am afraid that I might never see Portscatho again.

FIFTY ONE – LAST CHAPTER

And now my story is almost at an end; I feel like weeping, but by the same token, I feel victorious. Oh, my poor, tired brain, why do you have to play such tricks on me? I think you have won the race. As the years have gone by I have become increasingly aware of how my husband's role has subtlety altered. I remember four or five years ago, I wrote an article about my illness. In it, I had commented, that my husband was not my carer but he cared for me. However, now his role has slowly changed. Yes, my lovely Christopher still cares for me, but in addition he has had to learn to be a carer also. I look at my dog lying on the rug, next to me. He does not care that I have Alzheimer's or that I have just put my cup of tea in a draw.

Charting the changes in my condition has been a fraught journey. It has been a race against time. My book has been one of love and sometimes frustration and, at all times, the truth. It has resurrected many memories, sometimes sad, sometimes joyous.

And now my memoir is almost nearing its end. I think to myself how curious life is; a veritable mixture of disparate thoughts and emotions, some with no connection to the others; and from outside the window the birds are murky grey, shivering from the bird table, and fighting over a worm. We are no different, are we? We fight; we laugh; we cry; and we resolve our differences in one way or the other. Our little lives are of small consequence.

Since the pandemic I have been using modern technology, which of course I hate, but in fact, it has been a God-send.

Thus, I have been able to see my brother in Israel, and his family, without budging from my seat. And I light the candles which usher in Shabbat. I watch as my brother recites the prayers, with meaningful solemnity. I feel so close to him in this moment: I want to cry. So much has happened in the last few years. He blesses the wine and the bread. The prayers are timeless, intimate.

You can always find the beauty in any situation.
Take a feather and blow on it and watch it dance.

Lightning Source UK Ltd.
Milton Keynes UK
UKHW022017170622
404590UK00007B/818

9 781919 611433